THE KING OF MAGNETIC DREAMS

WEAVING VISION INTO REALITY

SURUCHI PURWAR

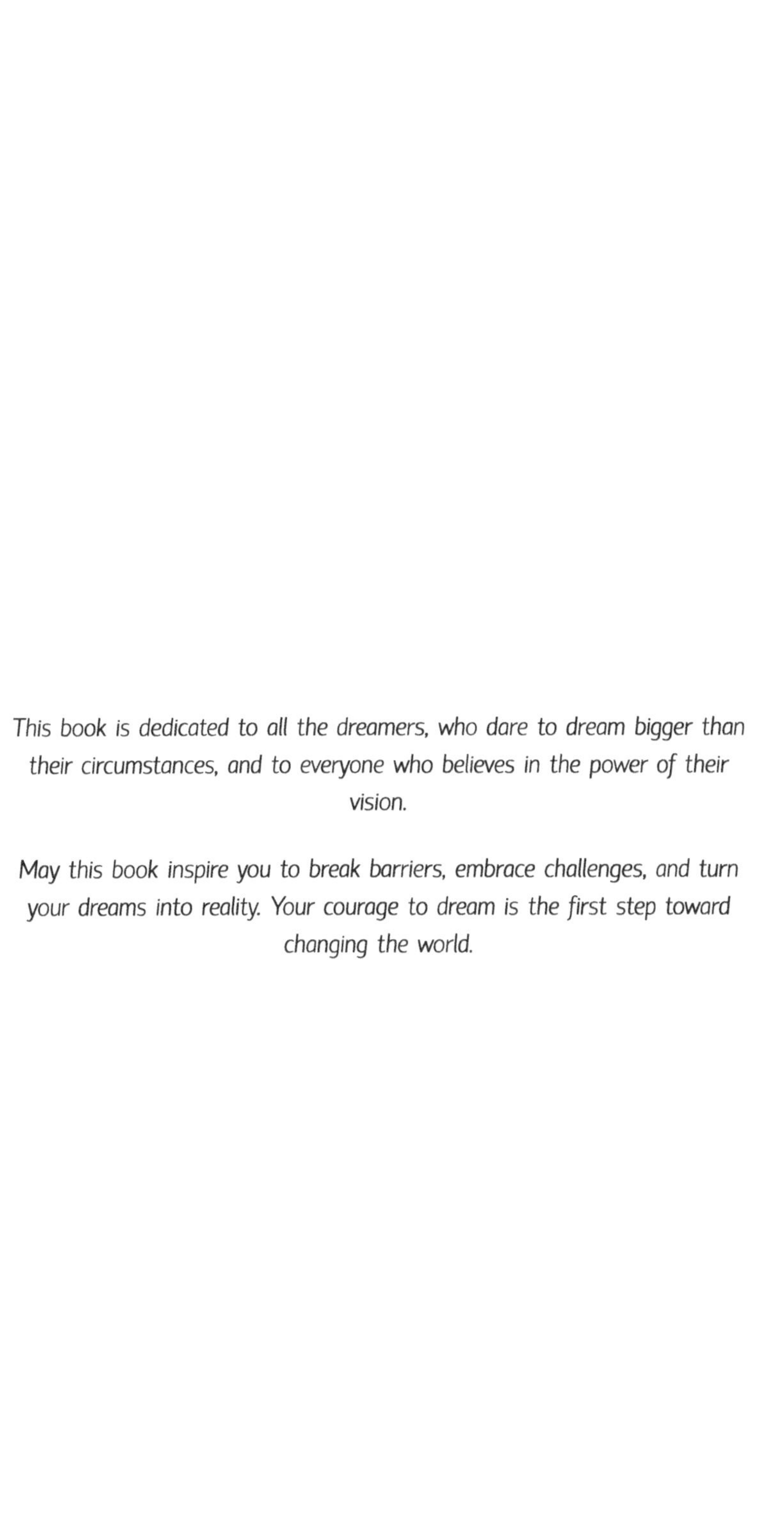

This book is dedicated to all the dreamers, who dare to dream bigger than their circumstances, and to everyone who believes in the power of their vision.

May this book inspire you to break barriers, embrace challenges, and turn your dreams into reality. Your courage to dream is the first step toward changing the world.

Contents

Contents

All Birds Find Shelter During A Rain,

But Eagle Avoids Rain by Flying Above the Clouds.

"Problems Are Common, But Attitude Makes The Difference"
~ Dr. APJ Abdul Kalam

Preface

What drives a person to defy the odds, break through barriers, and build a legacy that inspires countless others? Is it sheer ambition, relentless resilience, or an unshakable belief in the impossible? These questions stayed with me as I discovered the story of Aman Singh—a young man whose life is not just a journey but a testament to the power of magnetic dreams.

The King of Magnetic Dreams was born from a deep desire to capture the essence of a story that refuses to be ordinary. Aman's life is not a straight path to success—it's a maze of challenges, failures, and moments where the world seemed to conspire against him. Yet, at every turn, his vision burned brighter. He turned setbacks into stepping stones, doubts into determination, and dreams into a reality that touches lives far beyond his own.

This isn't just a story of triumph; it's a mirror for every dreamer. It's a reminder that no matter where you start, no matter how impossible the journey seems, your dreams have the power to reshape your destiny.

As you read, you'll uncover not only Aman's story but also the secrets that lie within each of us—the potential to lead, to create, and to make an impact that lasts. My hope is that this book stirs something deep within you, a whisper that says: "If he can do it, why not me?"

Dare to find out.

Suruchi Purwar
December 2024

Prologue

Every dream, no matter how big or small, starts with a spark—a quiet whisper in the heart that grows louder, urging you to act. It's the idea that refuses to leave, the one that stays with you through sleepless nights and waking moments, calling you to pursue it no matter the cost. Some people think that dreams are for the lucky or the special few, but the truth is, dreams are for anyone who dares to believe in them. Dreams are born in the hearts of those who refuse to settle, who choose to look beyond their circumstances and see a future filled with limitless possibilities. This is what The King of Magnetic Dreams is about—a story not just of one man's pursuit of his dreams, but of the universal power of daring to dream big, break through limitations, and embrace the courage to turn those dreams into reality.

At the core of this book lies a simple but powerful truth: our dreams are the most potent forces we will ever encounter. They are not just fleeting thoughts or passing desires. They are the compass that guides us, the energy that fuels our actions, and the fire that keeps us moving forward, even when the path ahead seems unclear. The journey of chasing our dreams is not always easy, nor is it a straight line. There are twists and turns, detours, and setbacks. But it's in those moments of struggle and uncertainty that we discover our true strength, resilience, and determination.

This story, The King of Magnetic Dreams, is one of those journeys. It's the story of a young man who, like so many of us, had a dream that seemed too big, too far-fetched, and maybe even a little impossible. But what set him apart from the many who only dreamt but never acted was his unwavering belief in that dream, his refusal to accept anything less than its fulfilment, and his commitment to make it come alive. This is a story that proves that it's not our circumstances that define us, but our ability to stay true to our vision, to persist through failure, and to rise above the doubts that surround us.

When you read these pages, you will encounter a man who dared to envision a future where everything was possible, and who worked relentlessly to bring that vision into existence. You will witness his moments of doubt, his fears, and the times when he felt like giving up, but also the strength that came from pressing forward. It's a story of transformation, not just in the external world, but within. Every challenge he faced was an opportunity to grow, every failure was a lesson, and every victory was a reminder that dreams, no matter how large, can become reality when pursued with passion, focus, and an unwavering commitment to the bigger picture.

But this is not just the story of a single individual. It is a story for everyone who has ever dreamed of something more but hesitated to take the first step. It's for the person who has been told that their dreams are too big or too unrealistic, for those who feel stuck in their current circumstances, and for those who are afraid of failing. If you've ever wondered whether it's possible to make your dreams come true, if you've ever doubted your ability to create the life you envision, then this book is for you. It's a reminder that dreams are not confined to a select few; they belong to anyone who dares to believe that they are worthy of achieving them.

In these pages, you will learn the importance of persistence and resilience—the ability to keep going even when the road is difficult, and the courage to keep moving forward even when you feel like you've reached the end of your rope. You will also discover the power of vision, and how the strength of a clear, focused purpose can carry you through even the toughest challenges. Vision is not just about seeing a goal; it's about living that goal, breathing it, and letting it shape your decisions, your actions, and your mindset every day.

What makes this story even more compelling is the magnetic force of belief. Belief is a powerful thing. It has the ability to shape reality, to influence others, and to draw the right opportunities into your life. When you truly believe in your vision and in yourself, you become unstoppable. The world begins to shift around you, aligning in ways that seem almost magical. Opportunities you never imagined begin to appear. People who share your vision show up at the right time, and solutions to problems that once seemed insurmountable suddenly become clear. This is the power of belief in action. It doesn't make the challenges go away, but it gives you the strength to overcome them.

However, belief is not something that comes easily. It's not something you can simply decide to have and expect it to be unwavering. It is something that must be nurtured, tested, and proven through action. It's easy to believe in the possibility of something when everything is going well, but belief is most powerful when it's tested in the face of adversity. This book shows you how belief in your dreams is forged through the trials, the failures, and the moments when all seems lost. It's about building a mindset that refuses to give up and learning how to keep going when everything around you says stop.

Through the course of this story, you will also see the importance of embracing failure, of understanding that setbacks are not the end but rather the beginning of something greater. Failure is not something to fear or avoid; it is an essential part of the journey. It teaches us, strengthens us, and pushes us to be better. The King of Magnetic Dreams is filled with moments where the dreamer faces obstacles that seem impossible to overcome. And yet, every time he falls, he gets back up—stronger, wiser, and more determined than before.

This is the journey of a dreamer who understands that success is not just about the end result, but about the person you become along the way. Every challenge, every mistake, and every success is a part of that transformation. It is in the struggle that you learn who you are, what you're capable of, and how much you truly want your dream to become a reality.

And it's not just about individual success. As the dreamer begins to transform his life, he begins to inspire others to do the same. Dreams are contagious. When one person dares to dream, they awaken something in the people around them. Their belief spreads, and soon, what was once a single dream becomes a movement. A community of like-minded individuals who all believe in the power of dreams and who support one another in their pursuit of them.

This book is not just for those who are in the middle of their dreams or already achieving great things. It is for anyone who has ever thought that their dreams were too big or too impossible. It is for those who are just starting out and who may be uncertain of how to turn their vision into something tangible. It's for the ones who have been afraid to take that first step or who have faced rejection and doubt. It is for anyone who needs to hear that their dreams are not only possible but worth the effort it takes to bring them to life.

The King of Magnetic Dreams is a reminder that dreams are not just fantasies, but possibilities waiting to be realized. It's about the power of vision, belief, persistence, and most importantly, courage. The courage to dream big, to act on those dreams, and to keep going when the world tries to tell you that it's impossible.

As you embark on this journey through the pages of this book, remember that your own dreams are valid, they are worth pursuing, and they are worth fighting for. The challenges you face will only make you stronger, and the belief you have in yourself and your dreams will be the force that pulls you through even the toughest times. Your dream is waiting for you. All you need to do is take that first step and trust that you have everything you need to make it a reality.

So, let this story serve as the spark for your own journey. Let it remind you that you, too, are capable of achieving your dreams, no matter how impossible they may seem. The King of Magnetic Dreams is here to inspire you to dream bigger, to go further, and to keep believing in the power of your vision. Your dreams are just beginning.

• XV •

@Suruchi Purwar

About The Author

Suruchi Purwar is an artist and the visionary behind *Ranggat*, an Indian art brand that lives by the mantra, "An Art from Soul." In 2023, she etched her name into history by earning both a Harvard World Record and an India Book of Record for creating the largest dot mandala art—a mesmerising 13x1 meter canvas masterpiece.

A passionate reader, Suruchi draws inspiration from the pages of books that fuel her creativity and determination. Her favorites, including *The Power of Positive Thinking*, *Lean In*, *Change Makers*, *The Habit of Winning*, and *Ikigai*, have shaped her perspective on life and success, nurturing her journey as both an artist and a writer.

For Suruchi, dreaming big isn't just an idea—it's a way of life. She firmly believes in the power of breaking through mental barriers and tapping into the inner strength that drives us forward. To her, every vision is a seed, waiting to grow into something extraordinary with the right mix of focus, persistence, and purpose. It's not enough to simply imagine the future—Suruchi is committed to crafting it, molding it with courage and an unwavering determination to reach her highest potential. Her art, her words, and her journey reflect her relentless pursuit of making dreams a vivid, tangible reality.

Who Is Aman Singh

Aman, a kind of person you notice the moment he walks into a room—tall, confident, and radiating an energy that feels both magnetic and reassuring. But it's not just his striking appearance or easy charm that draws people in. It is the way he listens, the way he speaks, and the way he makes you feel like your dreams, no matter how big or wild, are worth chasing.

Aman Singh is the founder of Rodez Web Technologies, a young man driven by a vision so clear it is contagious. He is not just a leader—he is a builder of dreams, a motivator, and a living example of what it means to dream fearlessly and act with purpose. For those lucky enough to cross his path, Aman is more than a professional—he's a source of inspiration, a guiding force, and a reminder that the extraordinary is within reach.

What fuels a man like this? What keeps him pushing through challenges with unwavering focus? What makes him believe in the impossible and inspire others to do the same?

This is his story. But it's also the story of those who've dared to dream alongside him, the lessons he's learned, and the vision that continues to grow. Keep reading, and you just might find a spark of your own.

What Is Rodez Web Technologies?

Rodez Web Technologies is more than just a digital solutions company—it's a launchpad for businesses ready to soar in the digital age. Specializing in web development, digital marketing, and cutting-edge online strategies, Rodez is where creativity meets technology to create impactful results.

Born from a vision to empower brands, Rodez crafts tailor-made solutions that go beyond the ordinary. Whether it's designing sleek, user-friendly websites, mastering the art of SEO, or building dynamic social media campaigns, Rodez transforms ideas into powerful digital experiences.

What sets Rodez apart is its unwavering focus on clients. Every project is a partnership, every strategy is personal, and every success is shared. From small startups to established brands, businesses trust Rodez to help them stand out, connect with their audiences, and achieve meaningful growth.

Fueled by passion and driven by innovation, Rodez Web Technologies isn't just keeping up with the fast-paced digital world—it's helping businesses lead the way.

Stragetic Partner

Aman Singh is a strategic partner to Suruchi Purwar. He plays a key role in managing Suruchi's art brand, *Ranggat*. Suruchi focuses on creating beautiful art, while Aman takes charge of building its online presence and shaping its business strategy. He handles everything from website development to social media, making sure *Ranggat* reaches the right audience and grows in a competitive market. His strategies and innovative ideas have been essential in helping the brand thrive.

What makes Aman's role even more special is the shared vision he has with Suruchi—a belief in dreaming big and making those dreams a reality. Working closely with Aman, Suruchi has seen his determination to overcome challenges and focus on the bigger picture. His drive and mindset are very similar to her own, and they inspire her to push her boundaries.

Aman's confidence in his vision for Rodez Web Technologies and his persistence in chasing his goals inspired Suruchi to write a book. It's a tribute to their shared passion for growth and their belief in the power of big dreams. Together, they show how hard work and a clear vision can achieve great things.

Suruchi's Perspective

As a writer, when I reflect on Aman Singh, I see more than just a successful entrepreneur or the founder of Rodez Web Technologies. To me, he exemplifies true leadership, vision, and integrity—someone who doesn't just build a business but nurtures relationships, cultivates creativity, and inspires others to dream big. His story is one that resonates deeply, not only because of the tangible success he has achieved but also because of the way he leads by example, turning every obstacle into an opportunity and every setback into a lesson.

Aman's journey is a remarkable blend of passion, determination, and an unwavering belief in his vision. What strikes me the most as I observe his path is the authenticity with which he pursues his goals. It's easy to think of leaders as people who know exactly what to do, who have everything planned and perfectly executed. But Aman's story reveals a different truth—that true leadership isn't about perfection. It's about vision and perseverance. It's about seeing possibilities where others might see limits and having the courage to act on those possibilities.

When I think about Rodez Web Technologies, I don't just think of a digital solutions company. To me, it represents something far more profound—an ecosystem where ideas aren't just discussed but brought to life. Under Aman's leadership, Rodez isn't just about developing websites or running digital marketing campaigns. It's about cultivating innovation, fostering creativity, and building a community where each individual can contribute to something larger than themselves. It's a place where relationships matter just as much as the technology itself, where the growth of the business is deeply intertwined with the growth of the people behind it. That, in my eyes, is what sets Rodez apart from countless other tech companies in the industry. It's not just a business; it's a movement, a collective effort to create something meaningful in the digital world.

As I observe Aman's approach to building his company and leading his team, I see a clear pattern: he believes in the power of people. It's not enough for him to build a business that serves a purpose; he is committed to building a team, a network, and a culture that supports, empowers, and encourages one another. He invests in his people, not just their skills but their dreams, their growth, and their success. This is why Rodez has become a thriving place of innovation—not just because of the cutting-edge services it provides, but because it's a place where everyone feels valued and inspired to contribute their best work.

From my perspective as a writer, Aman's story is more than just an inspiring tale of entrepreneurial success. It's a story of someone who doesn't take "no" for an answer, who believes in the power of connection, and who is always willing to go above and beyond to help others succeed. His vision for Rodez Web Technologies is rooted in a deep sense of purpose—he's not just building a company to make a profit; he's creating a platform for ideas to flourish, for creativity to thrive, and for relationships to be nurtured. He's transforming the digital landscape, not by following trends, but by creating his own path, one that others can follow and be inspired by.

What I find most captivating about Aman's journey is how it reflects the true meaning of leadership. He doesn't just lead with authority; he leads with humility, with a passion for his work that is contagious, and with a genuine desire to see others succeed. He doesn't just tell people what to do—he shows them how to do it. His leadership is about empowering others, building trust, and creating an environment where everyone feels encouraged to reach for their highest potential. As I write about him, I am reminded of the profound impact one person can have on an entire community—how one individual's belief in their vision can spark something extraordinary, creating ripples of inspiration that affect everyone they come into contact with.

As a writer, I find myself deeply inspired by Aman's ability to blend ambition with heart. He is a true visionary who understands that success isn't just about numbers, metrics, or accolades; it's about creating a legacy that goes beyond the surface. He's not interested in the temporary rush of instant success; he's focused on the long-term impact of his work, on the positive change he can make in the lives of others, and on the ripple effect his efforts will have on the world. His commitment to his team, his clients, and his community is what truly sets him apart.

Aman's story also highlights the power of believing in what's possible. It's not enough to dream; you have to act on those dreams. You have to take risks, face challenges head-on, and trust that the vision you hold is worth fighting for. That's something I admire deeply about him—his belief in what's possible, no matter how challenging the road ahead may seem. It's that same belief that has carried him through difficult moments and propelled him forward when the odds seemed insurmountable. In every conversation I've had with him, in every decision he has made, there is an undeniable sense of purpose—a belief that what he is doing matters, and that his work is part of something much larger than himself.

Through my eyes, as a writer, Aman's journey is a testament to the incredible power of dreams when they are fueled by action, vision, and dedication. It's a beautiful reminder that no dream is too big if you're willing to put in the effort and never stop believing in what you're capable of achieving. There's a certain magnetism to his story—a force that draws people in and makes them want to be part of his mission. It's not just about creating a successful business; it's about creating a movement, a community, and a culture that inspires others to dream bigger, think bolder, and live with purpose.

In writing this, I feel a deep sense of gratitude and admiration for Aman, not just as a leader and founder but as someone who has made a tangible difference in the lives of many. His passion, his commitment to excellence, and his unwavering belief in the power of people and connection are qualities that everyone can learn from. His story is one of triumph, yes, but also of struggle, of growth, and of the importance of staying true to one's vision no matter the obstacles.

Aman's journey is an invitation to all of us to follow our own dreams, no matter how big or small, and to trust in the power of persistence, creativity, and belief. It's a story I believe everyone should hear, because it serves as a reminder that with hard work, vision, and a little bit of heart, we too can create something extraordinary. It's a story of ambition, of resilience, and most importantly, of the transformative power of dreaming big and staying true to your purpose.

In the pages that follow, I hope you are inspired to see that your dreams, no matter how distant they may seem, are achievable. With a bit of courage and the right mindset, just like Aman, you too can turn your vision into reality. I feel incredibly fortunate to share his story with you, as it's a story that continues to inspire me every day.

Introduction

The dream that ignited a kingdom...

Aman & Rodez

In a world overflowing with ideas, it takes something truly extraordinary to rise above the noise. It takes a rare vision, a bold dream, and an unwavering determination to transform those ideas into something that leaves a lasting impact. This is the story of Aman Singh, a young and dynamic dreamer who didn't just imagine possibilities—he turned them into reality, shaping the digital world in ways few could have anticipated.

Aman's journey began not in a boardroom or a high-tech lab, but in the heart of someone who simply believed that technology could be a bridge to something better. His passion for both technology and creativity sparked a fire within him—a fire that would ultimately ignite the creation of Rodez Web Technologies. But what set Aman apart wasn't just his skills or knowledge; it was his ability to see beyond the horizon, to envision a future that didn't yet exist and set out to build it from the ground up.

Rodez Web Technologies wasn't just another digital solutions company—it was the embodiment of Aman's vision, his mission to reshape how businesses connect with their audience and grow in an increasingly digital world. From the very start, Rodez was built on more than just code and pixels. It was a space where innovation thrived, where ideas were nurtured, and where technology became the tool to help businesses reach their fullest potential. It wasn't just about creating websites or launching digital marketing campaigns; it was about crafting experiences, building relationships, and enabling businesses to truly stand out in a crowded online world.

What made Rodez special wasn't just the cutting-edge tech or the expertise of its team—it was the culture that Aman built around it. Under his leadership, Rodez became a kingdom of ideas, where every member of the team was empowered to think creatively, to dream big, and to push boundaries. It wasn't enough to simply meet client expectations; Aman's vision demanded that every project be an opportunity to exceed them, to innovate, and to redefine what was possible. Rodez wasn't just a company—it was a movement, a place where businesses could come to realize their dreams, connect with their audience, and achieve unprecedented growth.

Aman's personality was the spark that set this fire blazing. With his magnetic presence, sharp vision, and relentless determination, he didn't just lead by title—he led by example. His energy was contagious, inspiring everyone around him to push beyond their limits and dare to dream bigger. He believed in the power of possibility, in the idea that no challenge was insurmountable if you approached it with the right mindset. For Aman, failure wasn't an end—it was a lesson, a step toward something greater. His approach to leadership wasn't about giving orders; it was about inspiring those around him to take ownership of their roles, to bring their best ideas to the table, and to work together to achieve something far greater than any one individual could alone.

But what truly set Aman's journey apart wasn't just his technical expertise or his leadership style—it was his unwavering belief in the power of connection. While many companies were focused solely on the bottom line, Aman saw the true value in building strong, meaningful relationships with clients, colleagues, and partners. He understood that behind every website, every digital strategy, there were people—people with dreams, ambitions, and goals. And for him, success wasn't just about what Rodez could do for a business; it was about what Rodez could do for the people behind those businesses. He was passionate about empowering others, about helping them unlock their potential and achieve their dreams.

Rodez, under Aman's guidance, became more than a company—it became a platform, a space where innovation, creativity, and vision collided to create something extraordinary. It wasn't just about building digital solutions; it was about building a legacy, one that would continue to inspire future generations of entrepreneurs, dreamers, and creators. Aman's relentless drive to push the boundaries of what was possible created a ripple effect—an energy that spread far beyond the walls of Rodez, touching every person who interacted with the company, every business that partnered with it, and every dreamer who found inspiration in its story.

As Aman's journey continued, Rodez grew into a powerhouse of possibilities. What started as a small, passionate vision evolved into a thriving company that helped countless businesses find their voice, grow their presence, and connect with their audience in ways they never thought possible. But despite the success, Aman remained grounded. He never lost sight of the values that had led him to this point: vision, innovation, and the belief that anything was possible if you dared to dream.

This is not just the story of a business; it's the story of a dreamer who believed that the future could be shaped by the ideas we have today. It's the story of a dreamer and a self made visionary leader who dared to believe, who inspired those around him to push past their limits and embrace the power of possibility. And it's the story of a kingdom—a kingdom where ideas flourish, where creativity reigns, and where dreams are turned into reality.

Aman Singh's journey is proof that with vision, determination, and a little bit of courage, anything is possible. It's a story that continues to unfold, one that will inspire countless others to follow in his footsteps and create something extraordinary of their own. Because in the end, Rodez Web Technologies is more than just a company—it's a testament to the power of dreams, the importance of leadership, and the unshakable belief that with the right mindset, we can all build our own kingdoms of success.

Magnetic Dreams

The dream that ignited a kingdom...

Magnetic dreams are not just ordinary hopes or wishes—they are visions so powerful and captivating that they seem to pull people, opportunities, and success toward them. These dreams are different. They're bold, they're inspiring, and they carry a deep sense of purpose that lights a fire in everyone who comes near them. When you have a magnetic dream, it's not just your dream anymore. It becomes a force that attracts others, motivating them to take action, to believe in something bigger, and to chase after their own dreams.

Imagine a dream so compelling that it doesn't just stay in your head but becomes something real, something that others can see, feel, and connect with. That's what a magnetic dream does—it takes shape in the world around you, leaving an imprint that changes everything it touches. It isn't just about achieving something for yourself; it's about creating a ripple effect that pushes others to reach higher, work harder, and believe in the extraordinary.

At the core of every magnetic dream is a unique combination of passion, persistence, and the unwavering belief that anything is possible. It's the kind of dream that refuses to stay small. It challenges limits, breaks barriers, and keeps growing, no matter the obstacles in its path. The dreamer behind it may face setbacks, but the magnetic dream itself keeps calling them forward, pushing them to continue the journey, no matter how tough it gets.

What makes a magnetic dream even more special is its ability to inspire others. It's not just a personal ambition—it becomes a shared vision, one that invites others to join the journey. As the dreamer moves forward, they bring others along, encouraging them to dream bigger and take bold steps toward their own success. The magnetic dream creates a collective energy, a community of dreamers all working together, supporting each other, and helping each other grow.

It's a vision that doesn't just belong to the person who dreams it—it becomes a journey of growth and transformation for everyone involved. And in the end, it's the kind of dream that leaves a legacy, one that continues to inspire and guide long after the dreamer has achieved their goals. Magnetic dreams are the dreams that change lives, shape futures, and prove that with passion, persistence, and belief, anything is possible.

The Seed of a Dream

"where hope takes flight"

Aman's Early Life

Aman Singh's story began on February 14th, 1998, in a small town of Raebareli, Uttar Pradesh. Born into a family rooted in tradition, values, and a strong sense of pride, Aman was raised as a true Thakur boy, a title he carried with confidence, passion, and, yes, a bit of an attitude. From a young age, his personality radiated a magnetic energy that attracted people to him—his friends, his family, and even those who simply crossed his path.

But there was more to this young boy than just his charm and natural confidence. He was a dreamer—a thinker—someone who, even as a child, could see the world in ways others couldn't. As a boy, Aman was filled with curiosity and an unquenchable thirst for knowledge. Whether it was football, video games, or spending hours tinkering with computers, he was always on the move, trying to learn, explore, and discover something new.

A Playful and Artistic Childhood

Aman's childhood wasn't one of solitude and seriousness; it was full of laughter, adventure, and creativity. He had a mischievous side—a side that would often get him into trouble with his siblings and parents—but that same energy would drive him to explore new things. While football and video games were his outdoor and competitive pursuits, Aman also had a softer, more artistic side. He loved to sketch. There was something magical about capturing a moment on paper, creating stories, and expressing his thoughts in ways words couldn't.

But it wasn't just the art that sparked his creativity. It was the people in his life. His grandfather, *Shri Jagdamba Singh,* was his hero. A kind and generous soul, his grandfather was a living example of compassion and grace. Some of Aman's fondest memories were spent by his grandfather's side, listening to stories, learning lessons in humility, and watching him work with patience. It wasn't just the man he admired, it was his wisdom, his understanding of life, and the warmth he radiated that left a lasting impact on young Aman.

Aman's bond with his siblings—his younger brother Ayush and little sister Ayushi—was another defining feature of his childhood. They were his partners in crime, his sounding boards, and his biggest fans. The love, laughter, and closeness shared between them set the foundation for the family-oriented man Aman would grow into. Even in his mischievous moments, his love for his family was clear. They were his rock, his support system, and the ones who helped keep him grounded.

Education and Commerce Journey

Aman's education journey began at **Lucknow Public School,** Raebareli, where his natural leadership abilities quickly became apparent. Despite his playful nature and tendency to avoid studying, he had an innate ability to rise to the occasion when it mattered most. Throughout his early schooling years, he never failed to leave an impression. His teachers and classmates alike were drawn to his energy and enthusiasm, even when he wasn't necessarily the best student on paper. But this wasn't a reflection of his intelligence—it was simply his rebellious nature, his ability to think outside the box, and his refusal to follow the traditional path.

When the time came to choose a career path, Aman made a surprising decision—commerce. It wasn't an easy choice for him, but it was one that would shape his future. As he entered his final year of school, he put his mind to the test. The result? He surprised everyone—including himself—by scoring an impressive 85% in his 12th-grade board exams. This achievement was a turning point for Aman. It was a signal to him and to others that when he committed himself to something, he could excel. The seeds of his future were beginning to sprout.

Close Family Bonds

Family played a crucial role in Aman's life. He was always surrounded by love and discipline. His father, **Shri Deependra Singh**, a dedicated computer teacher, was his biggest role model. His father's work ethic and commitment to his profession were traits that Aman admired deeply. From a young age, Aman watched his father's unwavering dedication to his work, and it inspired him to be just as disciplined and focused in his own life. His father's influence helped shape Aman's attitude toward hard work and his belief that success wasn't handed to you—it was earned through effort and determination.

But it wasn't just his father who shaped Aman's character. His mother, **Smt. Sunita Singh**, was his source of unwavering love and support. She was the calm presence in his life, offering him comfort and encouragement through every stage of his journey. She was always there to remind him that no matter how big or small his dreams were, he was capable of achieving them. The combination of his father's discipline and his mother's nurturing love created a powerful balance that gave Aman the strength to move forward, even when the road ahead seemed uncertain.

A Visionary From the Start

Even as a child, Aman had big dreams. He wasn't like the other kids who simply followed the crowd—Aman was always thinking ahead, always imagining what the future could look like. By the time he was in 6th grade, he had already envisioned something that seemed unimaginable at the time—he wanted to start his own company. He didn't just dream of success, he dreamed of creating something that would leave a lasting mark on the world. This dream took shape in the form of Rodez, a company that would one day become the foundation of his professional life.

At such a young age, Aman was already confident enough to share this dream with his friends, even going so far as to change his name to "Aman Rock Rodez." It was a bold declaration of his future goals—a promise to himself and to the world that he would make his dream a reality. His love for computers, combined with his fearless Thakurasi attitude, set the stage for the journey that would follow.

Higher Education and Growth

Aman's journey of growth continued as he pursued his higher education at **Amity University in Lucknow**. These years were transformative. They gave him the knowledge and skills he needed to bring his childhood dream to life. The professors he met, the peers he connected with, and the experiences he had all played a part in shaping the vision of Rodez Web Technologies. It was here that Aman's passion for technology merged with his leadership skills, helping him realize that he could turn his childhood dream into a tangible, successful business.

But university wasn't just about academics for Aman—it was also a time of self-discovery. He learned to balance his creative and artistic side with the technical and business-minded aspects of his persona. These experiences were critical in helping him move from the realm of dreamer to that of doer.

The Adventurous Spirit

While Aman's mind was always buzzing with ideas and possibilities, his heart was equally adventurous. He loved to travel, to explore new places, and to experience life beyond the walls of his classroom or office. His love for adventure and exploration was not just about seeing new places—it was about discovering new perspectives, new ideas, and new sources of inspiration.

Every journey he embarked on, whether it was a weekend getaway or a long trip, fueled his creative spirit. His adventurous side helped him break free from conventional thinking, allowing him to see the world through a fresh lens. It was this unique perspective that would later influence the way he approached building Rodez—innovative, bold, and always pushing boundaries.

The Dreamer with Creativity and Courage

Aman Singh's life is a perfect blend of creativity, courage, and an unwavering belief in his dreams. His Thakurasi confidence, his deep love for family, his passion for technology, and his artistic soul combined to create a unique leader. From his early days of sketching and dreaming of his own company to founding Rodez Web Technologies, Aman's journey is a testament to the power of dreaming big, staying grounded, and having the courage to take bold steps toward achieving one's goals.

Aman's story is not just about success—it's about the courage to dream fearlessly, to work relentlessly, and to inspire others along the way. It's about finding the balance between ambition and compassion, between innovation and authenticity. His story shows that the seeds of greatness are planted in childhood, nurtured through hard work and love, and harvested with perseverance and passion. This is just the beginning of Aman Singh's journey—a journey that continues to inspire, to challenge, and to create something extraordinary.

CHAPTER TWO

The Awakening

"a journey to self-discovery"

A Dream Unleashed

Aman Singh's journey to success was anything but typical. His path was not paved with straight A's, awards, or a clearly mapped-out future. In fact, as a child, he was often the opposite of what society would consider "successful." Aman's early years were filled with mischief, school truancy, and a lack of focus on his studies. His parents, especially, spent many nights wondering what direction his life would take. Little did they know that the same mischievous boy, the one who could never sit still in class, would one day grow into the visionary founder of *Rodez Web Technologies*—a company that would go on to change the digital landscape. But sometimes, the greatest dreams are born in the most unexpected places, and for Aman, it all began with a spark—a passion for technology and a dream that would shape his destiny.

The Early Struggles

Aman's school life was far from conventional. While other kids were busy studying or participating in extracurricular activities, Aman was more inclined to break the rules. He spent his days playing football, exploring video games, and often found himself wandering far away from his studies. His focus was elsewhere, as the classroom seemed far less interesting than the world outside it. His teachers and parents, concerned by his lack of academic interest, often wondered about his future. But in retrospect, those moments of rebellion were more about a search for something deeper—a passion that was waiting to be discovered.

Aman's father, a dedicated computer teacher, played an unintentional yet significant role in shaping Aman's future. While Aman wasn't yet interested in computers, his father's teachings slowly but surely planted the seed of curiosity. Though Aman initially dismissed the lessons, a growing sense of interest in technology began to take root in him, though he didn't fully understand it at the time. This small spark of interest would eventually turn into a raging fire, leading him to pursue a career in the very field he had once ignored.

Despite his reluctance toward academics, Aman had a hidden side—a creative one. He loved to sketch, jot down ideas, and imagine new possibilities. This creativity, combined with his growing fascination for technology, would eventually lay the foundation for what would become his life's work. But it wasn't until later that Aman would fully understand how these interests would combine to form his true calling.

The Birth of a Dream

Aman's turning point came when he was in 6th grade. At that stage, most children are preoccupied with their next school trip, football match, or just hanging out with friends. But for Aman, that year was different. One day, sitting in class, he had a sudden and powerful thought: *"I will build my own company."* It was a fleeting idea, but it felt real. It wasn't something that would be easily forgotten or dismissed. He didn't know how or when, but the thought stuck with him. Even at that age, he knew that this was just the beginning of something bigger.

In his mind, Aman named his future company *Rodez*—a name inspired by the French city of Rodez. To him, the name represented strength, power, and possibility. It was a simple name, but it felt like a king. It wasn't just a name—it was a vision of who he wanted to become. As he thought about his future, he realized that this wasn't just a childhood fantasy; this was his path. This dream became his compass, guiding him through the turbulent years ahead.

Aman was so excited by this vision that he couldn't keep it to himself. He rushed to tell his friends about his dream, explaining that one day he would build a company that would revolutionize the world. To make it official, he even changed his Facebook name to *Aman Rock Rodez*, a bold declaration to the world that he was destined for greatness. At that point, Aman didn't have a plan. He didn't know how he would get there. All he had was a dream, and that dream was enough to fuel his journey.

The First Step: Turning the Dream into Reality

The road to success is never easy, and Aman's journey was no different. In 2016, he took the first step toward realizing his dream. He was still very young, but he had already decided to make his mark. He designed a website for a local NGO, a simple project that earned him ₹3000. The amount was modest, but to Aman, it felt like a jackpot. It was a confirmation that he had what it took to turn his passion for technology into something tangible. This small success of delivering a website was the spark that ignited the fire of belief within him.

Although Aman was excited about his success, he still had a long way to go. At this stage, he lacked the structure and knowledge needed to take his dream further. He was driven, but the practicalities of turning his dream into a business were still unclear. He had the raw potential, but the path was not yet clear.

A New Beginning: College and Realizing His True Calling

In the years that followed, Aman decided to further his education. He pursued both his bachelor's and master's degrees at Amity University in Lucknow. During this time, he gained the academic knowledge and technical skills that would later help him in his entrepreneurial journey. However, despite his newfound education, Aman found himself at a crossroads after graduation. He joined Tech Mahindra, hoping to thrive in the corporate world and gain some experience.

But within just a month, Aman realized that corporate life wasn't the right fit for him. The office culture felt restrictive, and he quickly grew frustrated with the monotony. He was the type of person who thrived on creativity, freedom, and innovation, not on following a rigid corporate structure. The final straw came after a heated argument with his manager over work ethics. That moment marked a turning point in Aman's life. He realized that he was no longer willing to compromise his dreams for the sake of a stable job. He made the bold decision to quit his job and pursue *Rodez* full-time.

Building Rodez from Scratch

Leaving the security of a stable job was a difficult decision, but Aman knew he had to follow his passion. Without any guaranteed income or a strong client base, he jumped into the uncertain world of freelancing. His first few months were challenging—he had no established brand, no portfolio, and no safety net. He took on small projects, worked late nights, and did whatever he could to stay afloat. But even in the face of struggle, Aman refused to give up. Every project, no matter how small, was a learning experience. Slowly but surely, he started building his portfolio, refining his skills, and gaining experience.

It wasn't long before things began to change. As Aman continued to work hard, word of mouth spread, and he began attracting bigger clients and more challenging projects. The name *Rodez* started gaining recognition, and what had once been a childhood dream began to take shape as a legitimate business. Aman's belief in his vision had paid off, and his hard work was beginning to yield results.

The Power of Dreams: Shaping Your Future

Aman's journey is a testament to the power of dreams. His story is not one of overnight success or smooth sailing. Instead, it's about resilience, persistence, and the unwavering belief in a vision that kept him moving forward. Through his journey, there are several key lessons that can inspire others:

1. **Dreams Have Power**: A single dream can light a fire within you, giving you the direction and purpose to keep moving forward. For Aman, his dream of *Rodez* gave him clarity, guiding him through challenges and setbacks.

2. **Believe in Yourself**: There were many moments when Aman doubted himself. But his belief in his abilities and his vision never wavered. Self-belief is a powerful tool that can propel you toward success, even when the odds seem stacked against you.

3. **Hard Work Pays Off**: Success is not about luck or shortcuts. It's about consistent effort, learning from your mistakes, and never giving up. Aman's journey proves that hard work and dedication lead to great rewards.

Overcoming Challenges and Dreaming Big

Aman faced many mental and emotional barriers on his path to success. He could have stayed in his comfort zone, continued with his job at Tech Mahindra, and led a predictable life. But the dream of *Rodez* was too big to ignore. He had to break free from his comfort zone, step into the unknown, and face his fears head-on.

Along the way, Aman overcame several challenges:

1. **Self-Doubt**: At the beginning of his journey, Aman had no clear plan. He didn't know how he would make *Rodez* successful, but his belief in himself kept him going. He trusted that he could figure it out as he went along.

2. **Fear of Failure**: Leaving a stable job to pursue freelancing was a risky decision. But Aman didn't let fear control him. He saw failure not as something to fear but as an opportunity to learn and grow.

3. **Challenging Societal Expectations**: Society often pushes us to take the safe route—get a steady job, follow the rules, and play it safe. But Aman chose to carve his own path, even when others didn't understand his vision. He broke free from societal expectations to follow his dream.

The Power of Belief: Turning Dreams into Reality

Ultimately, the key to Aman's success was his unwavering belief in his dream. He didn't have all the answers, he didn't know exactly how he would achieve success, but he knew one thing for sure—he believed in himself and his vision. This belief turned his childhood dream into a thriving business. *Rodez* was no longer just a dream—it was a reality.

Aman's story teaches us that with belief, determination, and hard work, we can all achieve extraordinary things. We can break through the barriers that hold us back, follow our dreams, and create something incredible.

The awakening has begun—will you answer the call?

CHAPTER THREE

The Struggle Begins

"rising against the odds"

Aman Singh's journey with *Rodez Web Technologies* is not just a business story; it's the tale of an unrelenting pursuit of a dream. A journey that began with a single thought—*"One day, I'll build something of my own"*—and transformed into a thriving company that spans borders, impacts industries, and continues to push the boundaries of what's possible. But every great success story begins with a struggle, and Aman's journey was no different.

At the core of *Rodez's* success is the idea that everything happens for a reason. This philosophy, deeply embedded in Aman's mindset, would shape not only his approach to life and business but also how he overcame the countless obstacles that stood in his way. His story, like many entrepreneurs, began small, humble, and uncertain. But over time, with immense patience, persistence, and hard work, Aman transformed his dream into a global reality.

The Seed of an Idea

The journey began not with a grand vision or a large-scale plan, but with a quiet, personal spark—an idea that grew slowly in Aman's mind. He didn't wake up one morning with a detailed business plan. Instead, it was a thought that lingered in the back of his mind for a long time: *"I can build something meaningful, something big."*

Aman had always been different from his peers. He wasn't content with just following the conventional path of securing a stable job and living a predictable life. He had a deep curiosity for technology and business, and most importantly, a desire to make a real impact in the world. However, he didn't have all the answers from the beginning. In fact, when he first took on a project in 2016—building a website for a small NGO—it wasn't a lucrative venture. The payment was modest, just ₹3,000. But it was more than enough to ignite something inside him. That ₹3,000 was not just money; it was validation. It was the first step toward a much larger dream.

That single project wasn't just a job; it was proof that Aman had what it took to turn his passion into something real. He was no longer just dreaming—he was doing. And this was only the beginning.

The Challenges of Growth

As Aman took on more projects, the reality of entrepreneurship set in. It wasn't all smooth sailing. It wasn't glamorous. It wasn't an easy road. But each new project brought its own lessons, each mistake its own learning opportunity. From one project, Aman went on to handle five, then ten, and eventually fifty projects. Each project, no matter how small, pushed *Rodez* forward.

But as the projects grew in number, so did the challenges. The workload became more demanding, and the responsibility heavier. Nights turned into early mornings as Aman poured countless hours into building his dream. There were many sleepless nights when exhaustion overwhelmed him. So extreme was his fatigue that there were times he would fall asleep in his office chair, too tired to move.

But for Aman, fatigue was never a valid excuse. The dream he had was bigger than the exhaustion, bigger than the frustrations, and bigger than the obstacles. With each passing day, the vision became clearer, and with that clarity came the motivation to keep going. But success was not just about managing projects—*Rodez* needed a team.

The Need for a Team

Aman knew that in order to scale his business, he would need to build a capable team. A dream, no matter how powerful, requires a group of people who share the same vision and determination. However, building a team wasn't as simple as it seemed.

The task of finding the right people was more challenging than anticipated. It wasn't just about hiring employees; it was about finding people who believed in the same ideals, people who could work tirelessly to build something extraordinary. Aman faced countless obstacles in trying to build a team, some of which felt like personal setbacks. There were moments of doubt, where it seemed like the dream might remain just that—a dream.

But as time passed, Aman slowly found people who aligned with his vision—people like Mr. Atul Vaya, who would go on to manage the Vadodara and Bangalore offices, and Mr. Priyanshu, who took charge of the Dehradun office. These were key moments in the company's history, as they allowed Aman to focus more on the company's growth and strategy while delegating day-to-day operations to leaders who could steer their respective offices toward success.

The First Big Break

While the journey was difficult, it was also a time of learning. Each challenge, every tough client, every missed opportunity taught Aman more about business, leadership, and his own resilience. However, in 2021, *Rodez* hit a major turning point with its first big government project—a ₹12 lakh contract that would ultimately prove to be one of the defining moments of Aman's entrepreneurial journey.

At first glance, the project seemed overwhelming. It was huge in scope, demanding in its requirements, and had a tight deadline. The pressure was immense. This was not just another contract—it was an opportunity to prove that *Rodez* could handle large-scale, high-stakes projects. If successful, it would open doors to more significant clients and larger projects. But the challenges were numerous. The client had high expectations, and the requirements were complex.

Yet, Aman and his team threw themselves into the project. For a year, they worked tirelessly, navigating hurdles, overcoming setbacks, and pushing forward despite the obstacles. The project was not only financially significant but also a test of their capabilities. Would they succeed or fail? It was a daunting question that lingered over the team every day.

In the end, the project was completed successfully, and the impact on *Rodez* was immense. It was not just about the financial success of the contract; it was about the confidence it gave Aman. The success of this government contract proved to him and his team that they could tackle any challenge. It marked the beginning of a new phase for *Rodez*, one where larger, more ambitious projects were within reach.

The Evolution of Leadership

As *Rodez* grew, so did the responsibilities of leadership. Aman had started *Rodez* with a clear vision and the drive to make it a success, but now he needed to evolve into a leader. The challenges of leadership became apparent as the company expanded. It wasn't just about managing projects anymore—it was about managing people, setting the company culture, and ensuring that everyone within *Rodez* shared the same vision.

The need for effective delegation became even clearer. Aman had to move away from managing every little detail and focus on leading his team, setting the direction, and ensuring that the company stayed aligned with its goals. This meant empowering his team members, giving them the tools and the autonomy to succeed in their respective roles. It was a difficult transition, but it was also necessary for the company to scale.

Aman learned that leadership wasn't about doing everything yourself—it was about inspiring others, empowering them, and creating an environment where everyone could contribute to the company's success. He understood that to build a lasting legacy, *Rodez* needed to be more than just his vision. It needed to be the collective vision of a talented team, working together toward a shared goal.

Expansion and Global Reach

As *Rodez* continued to grow, so did its ambitions. The company had already expanded its offices within India, but now, it was time to think globally. The goal was no longer just to serve clients in India but to take *Rodez* to the global stage. The team was ready, and the resources were in place.

Rodez began to attract clients from across the globe—Australia, the US, Dubai, Canada, Morocco, Pakistan, Indonesia, and China. These international clients weren't just business opportunities; they were proof that *Rodez* had evolved into a global player. The world had begun to take notice of what Aman and his team had built.

But expansion came with its own set of challenges. Entering international markets wasn't as simple as opening a new office. It required understanding different cultures, navigating international business regulations, and maintaining the quality of service that *Rodez* had built its reputation on. Yet, through careful planning, adaptation, and the dedication of his team, Aman successfully led

Rodez into international markets, marking a significant milestone in the company's history.

Lessons from the Struggle

Aman's journey was not just about success; it was about learning from every challenge, failure, and setback. His journey teaches several key lessons:

1. **Starting Small, Growing Steadily**: Success is built on small steps. By starting small and gradually scaling, Aman learned that incremental progress leads to bigger achievements over time.

2. **Patience and Persistence**: There were countless moments when giving up seemed like the easiest option. But Aman's persistence and patience—combined with the belief that everything happens for a reason—helped him stay focused on the long-term vision.

3. **Building a Strong Team**: Aman's realization that a dream is only as strong as the people behind it shaped the way he built *Rodez*. Trusting the right people and empowering them was crucial to scaling the company.

4. **Learning from Challenges**: Every failure, every missed opportunity, and every difficult client taught Aman valuable lessons that made him a better leader. Challenges were not roadblocks but stepping stones.

5. **Leadership and Delegation**: As the company grew, Aman learned the importance of delegation. It wasn't about doing everything himself—it was about creating a team of capable leaders who could share the burden of responsibility.

6. **Adapting to Change**: The business world is ever-changing, and *Rodez*'s ability to innovate and adapt to new challenges allowed it to thrive. Innovation, for Aman, was key to staying

competitive.

Conclusion:

The Struggle is Just the Beginning

Today, *Rodez Web Technologies* is a thriving, globally serving over 400 clients across various sectors. But this success wasn't handed to Aman on a silver platter. It was earned through relentless hard work, a commitment to learning, and a belief that with the right mindset, anything is possible.

The struggle wasn't easy, but it was necessary. And while *Rodez*'s journey has already been remarkable, the future holds even greater possibilities. The story is far from over—if anything, it's just beginning. With an unshakable vision, an empowered team, and a relentless pursuit of excellence, Aman and *Rodez* are poised for even greater success in the years to come.

The Breakthrough

"rising beyond the struggles"

At Rodez, success isn't just measured by profits or numbers. It's measured by the depth of connections we build, the strength of the teams we form, and the lasting impact we create, Aman said. At the heart of this philosophy is Aman, whose vision and leadership have led the company to its breakthrough moments, reshaping the way business is done and how success is defined.

Here's how Aman emphasised and explained his points:

The Power of Teamwork: More Than Just Collaboration

Teamwork at Rodez isn't just about dividing tasks—it's about building unity, respect, and a shared purpose that propels the entire team forward. Under Aman's leadership, the idea of a cohesive, supportive environment took shape.

Shared Vision and Goals

Every member of the Rodez team is aligned to a singular goal: delivering the best results for clients. Every project, every small task, is tied back to this larger purpose. This isn't just a mantra—it's the thread that weaves us all together, ensuring everyone is on the same page and moving toward the same vision.

Mutual Respect and Empowerment

Respect is fundamental at Rodez. Every team member, regardless of role, is valued for their unique contribution. Aman fosters an environment where everyone's voice is heard and where every idea is given consideration. This mutual respect creates a space where team members feel empowered to share their thoughts and innovate freely.

Collaboration and Support

Teamwork goes beyond just working together on projects. At Rodez, it's about always having each other's back. From brainstorming sessions to facing challenges, collaboration is woven into the fabric of the culture. If a challenge arises, it is met as a team, with everyone sharing their expertise to solve the problem.

Leadership by Service

One of the standout features of Aman's leadership is the "inverted pyramid" approach. He places himself at the bottom, supporting and enabling his team rather than leading from above. This unique leadership style ensures that every team member feels supported and motivated, allowing them to give their best without hesitation.

Winning as One

At Rodez, success is a shared victory. Whether we're celebrating major milestones or overcoming difficult challenges, we celebrate as a team. There are no individual accolades here; it's always about collective achievement. This sense of unity, even in times of struggle, strengthens the bonds that tie the team together.

Building Strong Client Relationships: Beyond Business, It's Personal

At Rodez, we don't just work with clients—we partner with them. Our approach to building long-term relationships with our clients is grounded in trust, empathy, and a commitment to their success, he said. For Aman, clients are more than business partners—they're family.

Client-First Approach

Aman always emphasizes that Rodez isn't driven by money, but by the relationships we build. This philosophy reshapes the way we interact with clients. We're not just here to complete tasks; we're here to help clients achieve their deepest goals. We never say "this is out of scope," instead, we ask, "What can we do to make this better?" This mindset ensures that no client ever feels neglected or unsupported.

Long-Term Partnerships

At Rodez, we focus on building enduring relationships. We work alongside our clients, not just for them. The goal isn't just a single transaction but an ongoing partnership that lasts for years, where we offer unwavering support as they grow and evolve, he emphasised.

Trust and Transparency

Trust is the cornerstone of every relationship at Rodez. Clients can rely on us to be transparent, to set clear expectations, and to communicate openly. We don't promise what we can't deliver, and we always put the client's best interests at the forefront.

Personalised Solutions

Every client's needs are unique, and at Rodez, we tailor our strategies to meet those specific needs. This focus on personalized service ensures that our solutions are not only effective but transformative, helping clients navigate their own challenges and reach new heights.

Going the Extra Mile

We believe that true success is measured not by what we gain but by how much we help our clients grow. This commitment to going above and beyond means that we'll invest the extra effort, time, and resources needed to ensure our clients succeed, no matter the cost.

Building Loyalty

Clients stay with us not just because of the results we deliver, but because of the trust, care, and dedication we consistently provide. This focus on relationships has resulted in an extraordinary 98% client satisfaction rate—a clear testament to our unwavering commitment to helping clients thrive.

The Real Meaning of Success: Impact Over Profit

At Rodez, we measure success by the difference we make, not by the numbers we rack up. This focus on impact shapes every decision, every strategy, and every interaction.

Helping Clients Grow

Success for us is helping our clients grow. It's about solving their challenges in ways that allow them to reach new heights and achieve goals they never thought possible.

Creating Lasting Value

We are committed to delivering value—whether through innovative solutions, building stronger brands, or offering the guidance that enables clients to break through barriers.

Making a Difference

Beyond business, we aim to leave a positive impact on everyone we work with—the clients, the team members, and the communities we serve. Our goal isn't just to meet expectations but to exceed them in ways that inspire growth and transformation.

Building Relationships Over Revenue

Profit, for us, is a byproduct of our relationships. By focusing on the success and well-being of our clients, the revenue naturally follows. Our 98% client satisfaction rate is proof of this—relationships built on trust and care outlast any numbers on a balance sheet.

A Legacy Beyond Numbers

The impact we create is what matters most. Numbers may fluctuate, but the positive change we make—whether through empowering teams, transforming businesses, or creating lasting value—becomes our legacy. Our goal is to be remembered not as a service provider, but as a partner that turned visions into reality.

Culture is the Soul of Rodez

Rodez's culture isn't just a set of practices—it's the soul of the organization. It's what gives us life, drives us forward, and shapes every outcome. At the heart of it is a belief in respect, teamwork, continuous growth, and innovation.

Respect for Every Individual

At Rodez, everyone matters. Every team member's unique contributions are celebrated, creating an environment where individuals are motivated to give their best.

A Family-Like Atmosphere

The Rodez family extends beyond the team—it includes our clients. This deep sense of belonging and mutual care fosters loyalty, trust, and collaboration, ensuring that both employees and clients stay for the long haul.

Shared Vision and Purpose

Everyone at Rodez shares a common goal: delivering excellence for our clients. This shared purpose ensures that everyone, from leadership to team members, is aligned and working toward the same objectives.

Leadership by Service

In Rodez, leadership is about serving the team. By providing guidance and resources, Aman ensures that every team member has the tools they need to succeed. This creates an environment where leadership is focused on empowerment and support, rather than authority.

The Power of Teamwork

At Rodez, collaboration is key. Whether we're celebrating wins or facing challenges, success is always shared. This collective approach fosters unity and ensures that no team member ever feels isolated or unsupported.

Continuous Improvement and Innovation

Innovation is at the core of our culture. We're constantly learning, growing, and finding new ways to deliver better outcomes for our clients. This mindset keeps the organization dynamic and focused on the future.

Why Culture Matters

Culture is the driving force behind Rodez's success. It attracts the right talent, builds lasting relationships with clients, and creates an environment where everyone can thrive. It's what makes us different and sets us apart.

Dreaming Big: The Power of Vision

Aman's journey with Rodez is a perfect example of the power of dreaming big. His philosophy of bold visions, combined with willpower and resilience, has transformed Rodez into a company that doesn't just do business—it shapes industries and changes lives.

Dream Big, Dare Bigger

Aman often says, "Dreaming big is the first step toward greatness. The size of your dream determines the scale of your success." He believes that the only limits we face are the ones we set for ourselves, and that mindset has propelled Rodez to new heights.

Turning Vision Into Reality

Aman's vision wasn't just to build a company—it was to create an ecosystem where growth, collaboration, and innovation could flourish. Every step, every decision, was made with the goal of turning this vision into a reality.

Fear of Failure Holds Us Back

Aman understands the fear of failure, but instead of letting it paralyse the team, he encourages them to embrace failure as a learning experience. "Failures aren't the opposite of success; they are stepping stones to it," he often says. This perspective has helped the team overcome challenges and turn setbacks into breakthroughs.

The Breakthrough: Dreams, Willpower, and Impact

What makes Rodez stand out is its commitment to relationships, innovation, and a shared vision of success. It's about more than just achieving goals—it's about making a meaningful impact, one client, one team member, one partnership at a time.

At Rodez, we've learned that dreams are the starting point. They ignite our passions, challenge us to push boundaries, and inspire others to dream bigger. With unwavering willpower and a focus on making a difference, there's no limit to what we can achieve.

Aman's journey at Rodez is a testament to the power of dreaming big and taking bold actions. It's proof that when you dream with purpose and work with passion, success isn't just a destination—it's a journey that transforms everything in its path.

CHAPTER FIVE

The Power of Belief

"where hope meets action"

In every journey, belief is the compass that guides the way. It's the force that propels individuals to pursue their dreams despite obstacles, and it's the foundation of every great endeavor. At Rodez, the power of belief isn't just a concept—it's a lived reality, embodied by the leadership of Aman and the collective spirit of the team.

Aman's journey with Rodez is a powerful example of how belief in oneself, in others, and in the possibilities of the future can lead to extraordinary results. His unwavering belief in the vision of Rodez, and his ability to inspire that belief in others, has been the driving force behind the company's success.

Belief in a Vision: A Dream Turned Into Reality

When Aman first started with Rodez, the vision wasn't just to build another technology company—it was to create something transformative. He believed in the idea of a company that could not only succeed but revolutionize the way business was done. This belief was grounded in his understanding that true success is built on relationships, innovation, and a deep sense of purpose.

Vision as a Guiding Light

Aman's belief in his vision became the North Star for Rodez. Every decision, every step taken, was aligned with the larger goal of creating an ecosystem where ideas could thrive, where teams could collaborate, and where clients could achieve lasting success. This belief in a better future for the company fueled every effort, regardless of the challenges that arose.

From Belief to Action

Belief alone isn't enough to achieve greatness. The real power comes when belief drives action. Aman's belief in Rodez's mission wasn't passive—it was actively pursued every day through hard work, resilience, and a commitment to innovation. This belief became a catalyst for every breakthrough, every new partnership, and every milestone.

Belief in People: Empowering Teams to Succeed

One of Aman's greatest strengths is his belief in people. He doesn't just see his team as employees or colleagues—he sees them as partners in the journey. This belief in his team is what has helped Rodez build a culture of trust, empowerment, and collective growth.

Trusting in Potential

Aman believes that everyone has untapped potential waiting to be unleashed. By fostering an environment of trust and support, he encourages his team to take risks, challenge themselves, and push beyond their comfort zones. He's always believed that the true

strength of Rodez lies in the individuals who make up its team, and he's made it his mission to help them realize their fullest potential.

Empowerment Through Belief

The power of belief manifests in how it empowers others. Aman's leadership isn't about telling his team what to do—it's about giving them the tools, the autonomy, and the encouragement to do it themselves. This belief in his team's abilities has cultivated a sense of ownership, accountability, and pride in the work they do.

A Culture of Confidence

When a leader believes in their team, it instills confidence in the entire organization. At Rodez, this belief isn't just top-down; it's mutual. Team members believe in one another, support each other, and are invested in each other's success. This collective belief in the potential of the team has been one of the key factors in Rodez's continued success.

Belief in Clients: Building Relationships That Last

For Aman, belief in his clients is just as important as belief in his team. Rodez's philosophy isn't just to provide a service—it's to build lasting partnerships based on trust, respect, and shared values. Aman's belief in the clients' potential to succeed has helped shape the company's approach to customer relationships.

Belief in Partnership

Aman views clients not as transactions but as long-term partners in growth. He believes in their vision and goals as much as his own, and this shared belief forms the foundation of every relationship. By treating clients as true partners, Rodez has been able to foster a deep sense of loyalty and mutual respect.

Empathy and Understanding

Belief in clients goes beyond simply trusting in their goals—it's about understanding their needs, challenges, and aspirations. Aman's ability to empathise with clients has created a space for open, honest communication, where clients feel heard and understood. This belief in their success fuels Rodez's dedication to going above and beyond, ensuring that clients always feel supported.

Transforming Client Success

By believing in the success of its clients, Rodez doesn't just deliver results—they deliver transformations. Whether it's helping clients streamline operations, build stronger brands, or navigate complex challenges, Rodez's belief in their clients' potential has been integral to achieving extraordinary outcomes. This belief in client success is what drives Rodez to consistently exceed expectations.

Belief in Innovation: Pushing the Boundaries of Possibility

In the ever-evolving world of technology, belief in innovation is essential. Aman's belief in the power of creativity and progress has shaped Rodez's culture of continuous improvement and cutting-edge solutions. At Rodez, innovation isn't just about staying ahead of the competition—it's about changing the game entirely.

Belief in Change

Aman has always believed that change is not something to be feared, but something to be embraced. He sees it as an opportunity for growth, discovery, and improvement. This belief in the power of change has helped Rodez remain agile, adaptable, and forward-thinking, even in the face of rapid technological advances.

Creating a Culture of Innovation

Belief in innovation isn't just about having a few groundbreaking ideas—it's about creating an environment where new ideas are constantly being nurtured and tested. At Rodez, innovation is a core value, and the company's success is a testament to the power of this belief. By encouraging creativity, experimentation, and risk-taking, Aman has cultivated a culture where innovation thrives.

Turning Belief Into Breakthroughs

Innovation at Rodez isn't just about technological advances—it's about finding new ways to solve problems and add value for clients. The company's belief in innovation has led to breakthroughs that have helped clients achieve things they never thought possible. Whether through new software solutions, business strategies, or marketing tactics, Rodez's belief in pushing boundaries has yielded powerful results.

The Ripple Effect: Belief in the Greater Good

The power of belief extends beyond the walls of Rodez. Aman believes that true success isn't just about building a profitable company—it's about creating a lasting legacy of positive change.

Belief in Social Impact

Aman's belief in doing good is reflected in Rodez's commitment to social responsibility. The company is dedicated to using its resources and influence to support causes that matter—whether it's through environmental sustainability initiatives, community outreach programs, or supporting charitable organizations. This belief in the greater good drives Rodez's efforts to make a positive impact in the world.

Inspiring Others

When people see a leader who believes in the potential of others, it inspires them to believe in themselves. Aman's belief in the power of dreams, innovation, and teamwork has inspired countless others to pursue their own passions and create change in their own lives. Rodez's success is not just measured by its growth—but by the positive impact it has on the people it touches.

The True Power of Belief: A Legacy of Growth and Transformation

Belief is more than just a mindset—it's a force that shapes actions, drives results, and creates lasting change. For Aman and Rodez, belief has been the cornerstone of every success. It has powered the company's growth, shaped its culture, and transformed the lives of everyone involved.

The power of belief is the belief in possibilities. It's the belief in people, in innovation, in collaboration, and in the future. And it's the driving force behind everything that Rodez has accomplished—and everything it will continue to accomplish.

Belief in oneself, in others, and in the greater good has not only shaped Rodez's journey, but it has inspired others to take bold steps, chase their own dreams, and build something extraordinary. In the world of Rodez, belief isn't just a concept—it's the foundation for everything we do, and the key to making the impossible, possible

CHAPTER SIX

The Setbacks

"the foundation of growth"

Aman Singh's life has always been about dreaming big. But dreams are not easy to achieve. They come with struggles, failures, and lessons that test a person's strength. Aman's journey was no different. He faced many setbacks that could have stopped him, but instead, they made him stronger.

An Idea No One Believed In

Aman's first business idea was something close to his heart. He wanted to build an online platform that would help people to sell their products to a wider market. He believed it could change lives, but the world didn't see it the same way.

When he pitched his idea to investors, most of them turned him down. Some said, *"It's not a good idea,"* while others doubted his ability to succeed. But instead of giving up, Aman decided to move forward on his own. With little money and limited resources, he started working on the platform by himself, often staying up late at night to get things done.

When Things Didn't Work Out

Despite all his hard work, the platform didn't succeed. It didn't get enough clients, and Aman couldn't find the funds to improve it. Eventually, he had no choice but to stop working on it.

This was a hard moment for Aman. He had poured his heart and soul into the project, only to see it fail. For a while, he felt lost and questioned whether he was even meant to be an entrepreneur. But Aman wasn't the kind of person to give up so easily.

He sat down and thought about everything that went wrong. He realized he had made mistakes, like not planning well enough and trying to do too much with too little. Instead of feeling defeated, he decided to learn from those mistakes and try again.

Fighting Doubts and Bias

As Aman worked on rebuilding, he faced another challenge: people's doubts about him. Coming from a small town with no elite education or big connections, Aman often felt underestimated.

People told him, "You should focus on smaller projects. People like you can't compete in big markets."

Those words could have broken his confidence, but Aman didn't let them. He believed in his vision and knew that his background wasn't a limitation. If anything, it made him more determined to succeed.

The Importance of Family

Through all of these challenges, Aman always stayed close to his family. His parents were his biggest supporters. They believed in him even when others didn't, and their love gave him the strength to keep going.

Aman's parents would often remind him, *"No matter what happens, remember where you come from and stay true to yourself."* These words stayed with him and guided him through every tough decision.

Even with his busy schedule, Aman always made time for his family. For him, they were his foundation, and no amount of success could ever come before them.

The Toughest Test

Just as Aman's company, Rodez Web Technologies, started growing, the economy hit a rough patch. Clients pulled out, and funding became harder to find. Aman faced some of the most struggling days of his career.

But Aman didn't give up. He focused on smaller, manageable projects to keep the company going. Slowly but surely, things began to improve, and Rodez emerged stronger than before.

Here are some potential setbacks Aman Singh might have faced:

1. Limited Resources in the Beginning

Starting with minimal resources—be it financial, educational, or network-related—is often a significant challenge. Aman may have had to overcome these constraints by relying on creativity, resourcefulness, and sheer determination to carve a path forward.

2. Navigating Failures

Many successful entrepreneurs experience failure, whether in business ventures, strategies, or partnerships. Aman likely faced moments where plans didn't work out as envisioned, forcing him to reevaluate and adapt his approach.

3. Skepticism and Doubt

Coming from a humble background, Aman might have encountered skepticism from others about his abilities or ideas. This external doubt, combined with any self-doubt, could have been a mental and emotional barrier.

4. Cultural and Societal Expectations

Balancing traditional expectations with a vision for innovation may have been challenging. Societal norms or familiar pressures to follow a "safer" path might have clashed with his entrepreneurial aspirations.

5. Building a Team and Trust

As a leader, Aman likely faced challenges in finding like-minded people to join his vision. Trust issues, differing work ethics, or early missteps in partnerships may have tested his resilience.

6. Overcoming Bias

Depending on his background, Aman might have faced biases related to his education, ethnicity, or social status. These biases could have made it harder for him to secure opportunities, investors, or partnerships.

7. Balancing Ambition and Personal Life

The relentless drive to succeed often comes at the cost of personal relationships and well-being. Aman may have struggled to maintain a balance between pursuing his dreams and nurturing connections with family and friends.

8. Economic and Market Challenges

Economic downturns, market instability, or competition could have posed significant hurdles in his entrepreneurial journey. Navigating these external challenges would have required strategic thinking and adaptability.

9. Emotional and Mental Strain

The pressure to lead, inspire, and succeed might have taken a toll on his mental health. Moments of burnout, isolation, or frustration are common setbacks for visionary leaders.

10. Criticism and Resistance to Change

As a change-maker, Aman likely faced resistance from those who were comfortable with the status quo. Criticism and pushback might have tested his resolve to keep pushing forward.

Despite these setbacks, what makes Aman Singh's story remarkable is his ability to overcome them, turning each challenge into an opportunity for growth. These struggles likely shaped him into a resilient, empathetic, and visionary leader. Would you like to explore how he addressed these challenges or how they influenced his leadership style?

CHAPTER SEVEN

The Overcoming Obstacles

"the strength to keep moving forward "

Every journey towards success is filled with challenges. These challenges test our resolve, patience, and determination. It's not the lack of difficulties that defines success but how we handle them. Aman Singh's journey at Rodez Web Technologies is a living testament to this. His resilience, unwavering belief in his vision, and adaptability have played pivotal roles in not only navigating challenges but transforming them into stepping stones for growth. His approach has shaped the culture of Rodez and inspired countless individuals to rise above their limitations.

The Simple Trick to Solve Problems

Aman's approach to problem-solving is rooted in the idea of a calm and collected mindset. Instead of getting caught up in frustration or panic when things go wrong, Aman takes a step back to clear his mind. He says, "If I can't find a solution, I take a break, play video games for half an hour, and then think with a cool mind. Every problem has a solution, and all it takes is patience and calmness."

This simple yet powerful tactic reveals a profound lesson: problems often appear more difficult than they truly are, and a moment of pause can help us gain the clarity needed to see the solution. Aman's emphasis on taking breaks highlights the importance of not pushing ourselves when we're overwhelmed. By stepping away from a problem and allowing our minds to reset, we can return to it with renewed energy and fresh ideas.

Key Lessons:

• **Patience and Calmness:** Under pressure, it's easy to let stress cloud judgment. A calm, clear mind allows for better decision-making and problem-solving.

• **Step Back to Move Forward:** Sometimes, the most effective way to solve a problem is to give yourself some distance from it, letting your subconscious work out the solution while you refresh.

Change Tactics, Not Dreams

Aman's belief in persistence is central to his approach. While he firmly holds onto his dreams and goals, he understands that the tactics to achieve them must evolve with time. "Dreams should never change, but tactics must evolve. When energy is low, think about your dreams to reignite your passion," he says. This reflects the idea that the road to success is rarely a straight line. Circumstances change, and setbacks occur, but that doesn't mean the dream is lost. It simply means that the approach needs to be adjusted.

This mindset has been crucial for Aman as he's faced numerous obstacles along the way. The constant adaptability of tactics ensures that the vision remains intact, no matter how difficult the journey becomes.

Key Lessons:

• **Adaptability:** While the end goal should remain constant, the approach must be flexible. Problems are inevitable, but finding new ways to overcome them is part of the process.

• **Momentum Drives Success:** Staying emotionally connected to your dreams, especially during difficult times, is what fuels your persistence and ensures you keep moving forward.

Overcoming Negative Thoughts

Aman acknowledges that during difficult times, it's easy for negative thoughts to take over and cloud our ability to think clearly. To counter this, he teaches the importance of replacing negative thoughts with positive goals. He says, "When your mind is filled with negativity, it's not easy to cut it off. You need a positive thought or a clear goal to replace and eliminate it."

This principle of redirecting focus is vital for mental resilience. Negative thoughts are natural in tough situations, but the ability to focus on what can be achieved, instead of what's going wrong, is what separates successful individuals from those who give up.

Key Lessons:

• **Focus on Positive Goals:** By directing your thoughts toward achievable and positive outcomes, you can shift your mindset and avoid getting stuck in negativity.

• **Replace, Don't Resist:** Fighting negative thoughts can sometimes intensify them. Instead, replace them with constructive, goal-oriented thinking to regain control.

Your Strengths Define You, Not Your Weaknesses

One of Aman's core beliefs is that success isn't defined by our flaws, but by our strengths. He says, "Don't waste time trying to fix your limitations. Focus on your strengths and let them shine. Everyone has cracks and flaws, but the real challenge is to find a way to use your unique talents."

This philosophy encourages individuals to recognize and leverage their strengths, rather than obsessing over their weaknesses. Everyone has areas they can improve on, but focusing on the unique abilities and qualities we already possess leads to greater success and fulfilment.

Key Lessons:

• **Embrace Uniqueness:** We all have something valuable to offer, and the key is to embrace our strengths, no matter how small they may seem.

• **Don't Let the World Define You:** Success is personal. It's not about conforming to others' expectations but realizing your own potential and using it to create something meaningful.

The Choice Between Success and Failure

Aman often speaks of the power of mindset when faced with challenges. In difficult times, people have two choices: to focus on past successes or to dwell on failures. He emphasizes, "In moments

of challenge, you have two choices: think about your past successes or dwell on failures. The choice is yours."

This idea reflects the importance of maintaining a positive and confident outlook. Focusing on past victories, no matter how small, helps reinforce the belief that success is possible. It also boosts morale and keeps the momentum going, while dwelling on past failures only drains energy and fosters a sense of defeat.

Key Lessons:

• **Learn from the Past:** Celebrating small successes reminds you of your abilities and reinforces the belief that success is achievable.

• **Focus on What's Working**: Concentrating on past successes helps you gain confidence, whereas focusing on failures can hinder progress.

The Role of Attitude in Triumph

When challenges seem insurmountable, the importance of a positive attitude cannot be overstated. Aman's mantra is simple: "When the pressure mounts, that's when you need to put your hand up and be counted. It's your attitude that makes the difference."

Resilience is built on attitude. In times of pressure and difficulty, it's easy to feel defeated, but Aman teaches that maintaining a positive attitude, even in the face of adversity, is key to overcoming obstacles.

Key Lessons:

• **Resilience Under Pressure**: The ability to persevere under pressure is directly linked to a positive attitude and mental toughness.

• **Step Up, Don't Step Back**: The most successful people are those who rise to the challenge, face adversity with courage, and keep pushing forward.

The Power of Patience and Persistence

Patience is often seen as a passive virtue, but for Aman, it's a powerful tool in achieving success. In the early days of Rodez, when he faced skepticism and doubt, his belief in the importance of persistence kept him going. Many questioned whether his dreams would ever become reality, but Aman's patience and belief in the process proved to be the key to success.

Facing Criticism: A Lesson in Strength

Criticism often comes when someone dares to do something different or ambitious. When Aman started building Rodez, he faced harsh criticism:

- Some doubted his abilities.

- Others dismissed his vision as unrealistic.

But instead of being discouraged, Aman used criticism as fuel to improve. He saw it as an opportunity to reflect on his actions, refine his approach, and prove his critics wrong. "Criticism, no matter how harsh, can play a huge role in improving performance. It pushes you to rise to your full potential," he says.

Key Lessons from Criticism:

• **Self-Reflection:** Criticism provides an opportunity to look inward and improve.

• **Building Resilience:** Each criticism is a test of resilience, and overcoming it strengthens your resolve.

• **Proving the Critics Wrong:** Aman didn't use criticism to fuel anger, but as motivation to prove that his vision could succeed.

The Power of Positive Expectations

Aman's belief in the power of positive expectations is fundamental to his approach. He says, "If you focus on failure, you attract failure. If you focus on success, you attract success." This mindset helped him and the Rodez team stay focused on solutions rather than setbacks.

When faced with challenges, such as a delayed project that threatened to lose a key client, Aman refused to panic. He kept his team focused on their strengths, fostering a positive outlook and a solutions-based mindset. This approach ultimately turned the situation around and earned the client's trust.

Struggles and Challenges: Nature's Way of Helping Us Soar

Aman often compares struggles to the process of learning to fly. "When you're struggling, it's nature's way of preparing you to soar to your full potential," he says. Challenges aren't roadblocks but stepping stones. They are there to prepare us for even greater achievements.

Aman's own journey with Rodez is a prime example. He faced numerous challenges—tight deadlines, limited resources, and self-doubt—but each struggle prepared him to handle the next one with even more confidence and wisdom.

The Wisdom of Standing Still

In some situations, the best move is not to act immediately, but to pause. Aman believes that standing still gives us the time to gain clarity and refocus. He uses the metaphor of walking on a thin log across a stream to illustrate this: if you focus on the fear of falling, you will fall. But if you focus on the goal, you will find your balance and make it across.

Final Thoughts

Aman's approach to challenges has been instrumental in the success of Rodez. His belief in the power of patience, persistence, adaptability, and a positive attitude has shaped the culture of the company and influenced the lives of those around him. His story shows that overcoming obstacles is not about avoiding difficulties, but about facing them head-on with determination and resilience. Success is not about the absence of challenges, but about how we respond to them. With the right mindset, any obstacle can become a stepping stone toward greatness.

CHAPTER EIGHT

Finding Balance

"navigating chaos and clarity "

In today's fast-paced world, where expectations are high and demands seem endless, finding balance can be a challenge. Many people think that success comes from working around the clock, pushing limits, and sacrificing personal time. But Aman Singh, the founder of Rodez Web Technologies, believes that true success doesn't come from burnout—it comes from finding the delicate balance between hard work, rest, and personal well-being. For him, balance is not an afterthought; it is a vital foundation for both personal and professional growth.

Aman's journey at Rodez is a clear reflection of how balance shapes success. As a leader, he has learned to not only manage the work demands but also the emotional and physical needs of his team—and his own. He has found that balancing the pressures of leadership with the need for rest, creativity, and team support is crucial for long-term success.

The Early Days: Learning the Hard Way

In the beginning, like many entrepreneurs, Aman threw himself into the business with complete focus. He worked tirelessly, often burning the midnight oil. His mind was always occupied with plans, strategies, and solutions for Rodez's growth. But after a few months, he started feeling the effects. The energy that once fueled his passion began to feel like a drain.

"I was so absorbed in the work, always thinking about the next step, the next challenge, and the next opportunity," Aman admits. "But I started realizing that I wasn't giving myself enough space to breathe. I was on a constant treadmill—pushing hard but not recovering fast enough."

This realization was a turning point. Aman began to understand that balance wasn't just about working hard; it was about making sure his personal well-being, and the well-being of his team, was prioritized just as much. As a leader, he knew that if he didn't take care of himself, he wouldn't be able to guide his team effectively. The early days taught him a valuable lesson: sustainable success isn't about sacrificing every other aspect of your life for work—it's about creating a healthy balance.

Key Lesson:

Energy and Rest Go Hand in Hand: Achieving success is not about working harder without pause, but about working smarter while also making time for rest, reflection, and rejuvenation.

The Power of Rest and Play

Aman quickly realized that taking breaks wasn't a luxury—it was a necessity. He started to prioritize activities that allowed him to unwind and recharge. One of his favorite ways to relax is by playing video games, something that might surprise some people who see him as a serious businessman. However, Aman sees the value in giving his mind a break and having some fun.

"Sometimes, when the pressure is too much, I'll take a break and play a game for an hour," Aman explains. *"It helps clear my mind, reset my thoughts, and I come back to work with fresh eyes."*

This approach is about more than just taking time off—it's about knowing what rejuvenates you. For some, it might be sports, meditation, or spending time with loved ones. For others, like Aman, it's finding something that allows them to escape temporarily from the stress of work and dive into something that brings joy. These moments of relaxation are essential in maintaining long-term focus, motivation, and creativity. Aman encourages his team to also find their own outlets, understanding that personal time is as important as professional commitment.

Key Lesson:

Rest Isn't a Waste of Time: Play and relaxation recharge your mind and body, which in turn helps you return to your work with greater energy, clarity, and enthusiasm. A balanced life leads to sustained productivity and creativity.

Leading with Empathy: Balancing Personal and Professional Growth

One of the greatest challenges for any leader is balancing personal goals with the needs of the team. As the head of Rodez, Aman is not only responsible for his own growth but for guiding his team to success as well. Over time, he began to notice that while his team was working incredibly hard, the pressure was starting to show. He wanted to create an environment where people felt supported, both as professionals and individuals.

"A team's success is built on the well-being of its members," Aman says. "I realized that I couldn't just focus on projects and deadlines. I had to make sure everyone had the space they needed to maintain a good work-life balance."

Aman implemented flexible work hours, encouraged employees to take vacations, and reminded everyone to take breaks during the workday. He regularly checked in with his team to ensure they weren't overwhelmed and emphasized the importance of mental health. This shift in perspective helped foster an environment of empathy, where people could thrive professionally without sacrificing their personal lives.

Key Lesson:

Leadership Is About People, Not Just Projects: Good leaders understand that their team's well-being is just as important as meeting deadlines. Creating a supportive environment allows people to grow and perform at their best, without risking burnout.

Patience vs. Urgency: Finding the Right Pace

Aman's leadership also involves finding the right balance between urgency and patience. In the business world, there are times when things need to move quickly, and decisions must be made in a rush. But there are other times when it's better to step back, reflect, and let things unfold naturally. This balance is crucial for maintaining long-term stability.

"When I first started Rodez, I was driven to get results quickly, but I quickly learned that sometimes rushing only creates more problems," Aman shares. "There's a time for urgency and a time to step back, wait, and let the pieces fall into place. The key is knowing when to act and when to be patient."

For instance, when Rodez faced a crisis with a key client, Aman was faced with a choice: he could push his team to work overtime to meet a tight deadline, or he could take a step back, assess the situation, and come up with a more sustainable solution. He chose the latter. By taking time to think, he helped his team deliver a solution that not only saved the client's trust but also maintained their health and morale.

Key Lesson:

Balance Urgency with Patience: The key to success is knowing when to move quickly and when to allow time for careful consideration. Urgency can drive immediate results, but patience leads to sustainable progress.

The Balance of Learning and Doing

Another aspect of balance that Aman values is the balance between learning and doing. He is always seeking new knowledge—whether it's reading books, attending workshops, or learning from others in the industry. But he knows that learning alone won't lead to progress. You must also take action and apply what you've learned.

"I'm always learning, but I also make sure that I apply what I've learned. Real growth happens when you put your knowledge into practice," Aman explains. "The balance between acquiring new information and taking action is what has helped me grow both as a leader and as a person."

Aman encourages his team to embrace both learning and doing. He believes that continuous growth comes not just from reading or attending seminars but from experimenting, testing new ideas, and applying knowledge in real-world situations.

Key Lesson:

Learning and Doing Are Two Sides of the Same Coin: Growth happens when you balance learning with action. Knowledge without application is incomplete. Putting what you learn into practice is the key to progress.

The Ongoing Journey of Balance

Aman understands that achieving balance is not a one-time task. It is an ongoing journey that requires constant attention and adjustment. Some days, work demands more of his energy, while other days, he focuses on self-care or personal goals. For him, balance is not about perfection—it's about being flexible and making sure that all aspects of life receive the attention they deserve.

Through his journey with Rodez, Aman has shown that success doesn't come from working harder or pushing yourself beyond your limits. It comes from understanding the importance of balance—between work and rest, urgency and patience, learning and doing. By making time for all aspects of life, he has been able to sustain his energy, creativity, and leadership in a way that promotes long-term success, both for himself and his company.

Final Thoughts:

Aman's journey teaches us that finding balance is the key to sustainable success. It's about understanding that you don't have to sacrifice one aspect of your life for another. By nurturing your work, health, relationships, and personal growth, you create a foundation that supports long-term achievement. At Rodez, this philosophy has shaped the way the company works and grows, creating an environment where both the business and the people behind it can thrive.

In the end, balance isn't just a strategy—it's a lifestyle. And for Aman, it is the secret ingredient to success.

CHAPTER NINE

The King of Magnetic Dreams

"weaving vision into reality"

In the world of business and entrepreneurship, some leaders rise through sheer skill and determination. But then there are visionaries like **Aman Singh**, who not only rise but also inspire others to follow, transforming their dreams into reality and making the impossible seem achievable. Aman is not just a business leader—he is a **dreamer**, a **builder**, and a **magnet for greatness**. His journey is not about simply reaching personal success; it's about creating a wave of transformation that touches everyone who enters his orbit.

Aman is admired as **"The King of Magnetic Dreams"**, not because of his ability to dream big but because of the unique force he has to draw others into his vision, to make his dreams their dreams. But what makes Aman's dreams so magnetic? Why do people—his team, clients, collaborators—find themselves inspired and moved to join him on his journey? The answer lies in his **vision, passion, resilience**, and above all, his **unshakable belief** in the extraordinary potential of others.

Let's dive deeper into the qualities that make Aman the King of Magnetic Dreams, and why his journey is one that not only deserves admiration but also serves as a powerful inspiration to dreamers everywhere.

1. A Visionary Leader Who Sees the Future Before It Happens

Aman Singh is the type of leader who sees the world not as it is but as it could be. He's a visionary in the truest sense of the word, constantly looking ahead to the future, to the vast ocean of possibilities. When he founded **Rodez Web Technologies**, it wasn't just about creating another tech company—it was about building an ecosystem where ideas would come to life, where innovation and creativity would be nurtured, and where technology could drive change in industries and people's lives.

Aman had an unwavering belief in the potential of Rodez, even when others were skeptical. The early days were tough, and many questioned his ability to build something sustainable in an already crowded market. But Aman's vision wasn't swayed by doubt; it was refined by it. He didn't just want to create a company—he wanted to **transform an industry**. Where others saw limitations, Aman saw **endless possibilities**.

Examples of His Visionary Leadership:

• **Turning Challenges into Opportunities:** During Rodez's early struggles, when others would have folded under the pressure, Aman used every setback as a stepping stone. Whether it was financial difficulties or market competition, he saw each challenge as an opportunity to innovate, pivot, and strengthen the foundation of his company.

• **Focusing on Long-Term Goals Rather Than Quick Wins:** From the very start, Aman emphasized sustainable growth over short-term profits. His approach was always about creating value for his clients, building long-lasting relationships, and growing slowly but steadily.

Why This Stands Out:

Aman's ability to see the bigger picture and think beyond immediate obstacles gives his team and clients the confidence to believe in the vision, even when things seem uncertain. His vision acts as a compass, guiding everyone around him toward a shared goal, inspiring them to dream bigger, think bolder, and achieve more.

2. The Power to Inspire: Sparking the Fire of Passion in Others

One of Aman's most remarkable gifts is his ability to inspire people—not just through his words but through his actions, his energy, and his unwavering commitment to his dreams. Aman doesn't just motivate others; he **ignites a fire within them**. His passion is contagious, and his belief in the potential of others is what makes his dreams so magnetic.

Aman knows that the true power of any business lies not just in profits but in the **people** behind it. His focus has always been on empowering his team, helping them recognize their strengths, and giving them the confidence to reach for their own greatness.

How He Inspires:

• **Empowering His Team:** Aman sees potential where others may see doubt. He doesn't just manage his team—he **mentors** them. He encourages each individual to tap into their strengths, challenge their limitations, and aim for excellence. His focus isn't just on tasks—it's on developing people to be the best versions of themselves.

• **Leading by Example:** Whether it's staying calm during crises or embracing challenges with open arms, Aman leads through action. His behavior sets the tone for the whole company. He doesn't just tell people what to do; he shows them how it's done.

• **Creating a Culture of Positivity and Collaboration:** At Rodez, it's more than just work—it's about a sense of belonging. Aman has fostered a culture that values collaboration over competition, respect over rivalry, and growth over stagnation. His positivity infuses everything, creating an environment where everyone feels valued and empowered to contribute.

Impact of His Inspiration:

What makes Aman's ability to inspire so powerful is that his influence doesn't stop with just one person—it's collective. His passion and vision are contagious. His team, his clients, and his collaborators don't just buy into his dreams—they make them their own. What began as Aman's vision for Rodez becomes a shared mission that everyone works toward, fueled by the common belief that they are part of something greater.

3. Relentless Passion for Excellence: No Compromise, Only Growth

For Aman, **excellence is not negotiable.** Mediocrity doesn't have a place in his world. He constantly strives to do the best he can, and this passion for perfection ripples through everything he touches. From the quality of the work produced by his team to the relationships he cultivates with clients, Aman's commitment to excellence drives him to go above and beyond, always seeking ways to improve and grow.

This passion for excellence isn't just about pushing his company to greater heights—it's about leading by example and inspiring those around him to match his energy and enthusiasm for continuous improvement.

Examples of His Passion:

• **Attention to Detail:** In the world of technology and business, small things matter. Aman's attention to detail is meticulous. He ensures that every project, every task, and every relationship is handled with the utmost care and dedication, no matter how small it may seem.

• **Pursuit of Growth:** Aman is always looking for the next step. Whether it's refining a process, learning a new skill, or expanding his company's reach, his hunger for growth is insatiable. For him, the pursuit of excellence is not a one-time goal—it's a continuous journey.

Why This Matters:

Aman's commitment to excellence sets the standard for everyone at Rodez. When he expects the best, he gets the best. His dedication pushes his team to reach higher, aim further, and deliver more, creating a culture of excellence that permeates every level of the organization.

4. Resilience and Positivity: Turning Adversity into Triumph

Every leader faces obstacles—but not every leader has the resilience to turn those obstacles into triumphs. Aman's journey has been far from smooth, filled with challenges that would have made most people give up. But instead of shrinking from adversity, Aman embraces it. He doesn't just endure hardship—he grows from it.

Aman's philosophy is simple yet powerful: **"Every problem comes with a solution; you just need patience and a calm mind."** His ability to stay calm under pressure, think strategically, and persevere has been a cornerstone of Rodez's success.

Examples of Resilience:

• **Facing Criticism:** In the beginning, many doubted Aman's ability to turn his vision into reality. But instead of feeling discouraged, Aman used those doubts as fuel to prove them wrong. He didn't just listen to criticism—he turned it into a driving force for improvement.

• **Overcoming Setbacks:** Whether it was a financial struggle or a logistical challenge, Aman's resilience kept him focused on the bigger picture. He stayed calm, assessed the situation, and found a way forward. His ability to reset his mind and look for solutions, rather than dwelling on problems, has been key to Rodez's ability to bounce back stronger each time.

Why This Defines Him:

Aman's resilience isn't just a personal trait—it's a source of strength for his entire team. When faced with challenges, his ability to stay positive and solution-focused inspires those around him to do the same. It creates an environment where setbacks are seen not as roadblocks but as opportunities to learn and grow.

5. A Magnet for Dreams: Attracting People, Opportunities, and Success

Aman has an uncanny ability to attract not just people but opportunities. Clients, collaborators, and talented individuals are naturally drawn to him, not just because of his **vision**, but because of his **authenticity**, **confidence**, and genuine care for others. He doesn't just chase success—he **magnetizes** it.

When Aman speaks about his dreams, people listen. When he acts, others follow. His belief in his vision is so strong, so infectious, that it inspires others to believe in it too.

What Makes Him Magnetic:

• **Authenticity:** Aman's dreams are not self-serving—they are about creating value and making a difference. This authenticity attracts like-minded individuals who share his passion for creating lasting change.

• **Confidence:** Aman's confidence isn't just about himself—it's about the future. When he speaks, people can see his belief in the possibilities of the future. This confidence instills a sense of purpose in others, making them want to be a part of his journey.

• **Empathy:** Aman has an incredible ability to understand and connect with people on a personal level. His genuine care for others builds deep, lasting relationships that create a powerful network of support.

Impact of His Magnetism:

Aman's magnetic energy doesn't just bring people into his world—it brings **opportunities**. Clients, partners, and talented individuals are naturally drawn to him, eager to work alongside him to turn his dreams into shared realities.

Lessons from Aman, the King of Magnetic Dreams

Aman's journey is a powerful lesson in the importance of dreaming big, staying resilient, and inspiring others. Here are the key takeaways from his remarkable story:

• **Dream Big, Start Small:** No dream is too big if you take consistent, deliberate steps toward it. Aman's journey shows that even the boldest ideas can become a reality with patience and persistence.

• **Inspire Others:** True success isn't just about what you achieve—it's about empowering others to achieve their best. Inspire those around you, and together you can accomplish extraordinary things.

• **Resilience Turns Obstacles into Opportunities:** Life will throw challenges your way, but resilience and a positive mindset can transform setbacks into springboards for growth.

• **Focus on Impact, Not Personal Gain:** Dreaming for the greater good creates lasting value. When you focus on making a difference, success follows naturally.

• **Build Strong Relationships:** The path to success is never solitary. The people you meet, the relationships you build, and the collaborations you foster are what will truly elevate your journey.

Why Aman is the King of Magnetic Dreams

Aman Singh is the **King of Magnetic Dreams** because he doesn't just dream for himself—he dreams for everyone around him. His vision is powerful, his passion is contagious, and his belief in others is unshakable. Aman doesn't just attract success—he creates it. His ability to unite people, inspire greatness, and turn challenges into triumphs is what truly makes him a magnet for dreams.

Through his journey, Aman proves that dreams are not just personal ambitions—they are collective missions that, when shared, have the power to change the world. And that's exactly what he's doing, every single day.

CHAPTER TEN

The Legacy in Motion

"building a future beyond today"

The journey of Aman Singh and Rodez Web Technologies is a living testament to the power of vision, resilience, and bold action. What began as an ambitious dream is now a thriving enterprise, impacting lives, shaping industries, and redefining possibilities. With every milestone, Aman and Rodez are building a legacy—a story of innovation, empowerment, and unyielding determination.

This legacy is not static; it's in constant motion, driven by Aman's ever-expanding vision and the unstoppable force of a team that shares his belief in greatness. From opening their fifth office in Bangalore to setting their sights on new horizons, the story of Rodez is just beginning, and the future promises even greater achievements.

A Vision Rooted in Growth and Impact

Aman's journey with Rodez has always been about more than just business. His vision is to create a company that not only excels in technology but also leaves a lasting impact on society.

1. **Building Opportunities:**

One of Aman's most ambitious goals is to make Rodez a company that employs **20,000 people**. This vision is not just about numbers; it's about changing lives. By creating meaningful jobs, Aman is empowering individuals, supporting families, and uplifting communities.

"Every job we create is a step toward building a better future—not just for our company but for the world around us," Aman says.

2. Expanding Horizons:

In 2025, Rodez will step into the hospitality industry with the launch of **Hotel Rodez** in Lucknow. This venture symbolizes more than just business diversification; it's a celebration of culture, hospitality, and connection.

The hotel will blend modern luxury with the warmth of traditional Indian hospitality, creating a space that embodies Rodez's core values of innovation, excellence, and a people-first approach. It will also serve as a beacon of opportunity, providing jobs and contributing to the economic growth of Lucknow.

3. Scaling Financial Heights:

Aman has set a bold financial target: to make Rodez a **100-crore company within the next five years**. Achieving this goal will require not only scaling operations but also partnering with global brands and delivering unmatched value.

This ambitious milestone is not just about financial success—it's about creating a company that stands as a symbol of trust, creativity, and excellence on the global stage.

Bangalore: A Strategic Leap Forward

The opening of Rodez's fifth office in Bangalore, often called the **Silicon Valley of India**, marks a pivotal moment in the company's journey. Bangalore is a city that thrives on innovation and is home to some of the brightest minds in technology. It's the perfect setting for Rodez's most ambitious project yet: a cutting-edge **AI-based initiative** designed to revolutionize how businesses use technology.

This new office isn't just a workplace—it's a launchpad for innovation. It reflects Aman's commitment to staying ahead of industry trends and positioning Rodez as a leader in technological advancement. The team in Bangalore will not only work on groundbreaking solutions but also play a key role in shaping the future of the company.

By choosing Bangalore, Aman has made a statement: Rodez is here to innovate, inspire, and lead.

Lucknow: A New Chapter in Hospitality

While Rodez is known for its prowess in technology, Aman's vision extends beyond a single industry. The decision to establish **Hotel Rodez in Lucknow** is a bold step into the world of hospitality, reflecting his belief in creating meaningful experiences.

Lucknow, a city known for its rich heritage and unparalleled hospitality, provides the perfect backdrop for this venture. The hotel will be more than a place to stay—it will be an experience, combining modern luxury with the charm of tradition.

For Aman, this project represents more than business growth. It's about:

• **Creating Opportunities:** The hotel will generate employment, from hospitality staff to local artisans, contributing to the city's economy.

• **Celebrating Culture:** By blending tradition with modernity, Hotel Rodez will showcase the cultural richness of Lucknow to a global audience.

• **Expanding the Rodez Brand:** This venture symbolizes the versatility and ambition of Rodez, proving that their legacy is not limited to technology.

Aiming for 100 Crores: A Bold Target

One of the most inspiring aspects of Aman's vision is his determination to scale Rodez into a **100-crore company** over the next five years. This goal is not just about financial growth—it's about creating value, building trust, and positioning Rodez as a leader in the global market.

To achieve this:

• **Onboarding Big Brands:** Rodez is working to partner with globally recognized brands, offering innovative solutions that meet their unique needs.

• **Expanding Service Offerings:** By diversifying its portfolio, Rodez is catering to a wider range of industries, from AI and e-commerce to healthcare and hospitality.

• **Investing in Talent:** Aman understands that a company's true strength lies in its people. By hiring and nurturing top talent, Rodez is building a team capable of driving its ambitious goals forward.

This financial target is not just a milestone; it's a reflection of Rodez's potential to become a global powerhouse of innovation and excellence.

Why This Legacy Matters

What sets Aman's journey apart is the **intent behind his vision.** His goals are not just about personal success or corporate growth—they're about making a difference. Every decision, every milestone, and every step forward is guided by a desire to create value for people, whether they're employees, clients, or the communities he serves.

1. Inspiring Generations:

Aman's journey is a source of inspiration for entrepreneurs, dreamers, and anyone who dares to think big. His story proves that with vision, resilience, and hard work, even the most ambitious dreams can become reality.

2. Empowering Communities:

By creating jobs, supporting local economies, and fostering innovation, Rodez is more than just a company—it's a force for positive change.

3. Leaving a Lasting Impact:

From technology to hospitality, Aman's ventures are designed to stand the test of time. His legacy is not just about what he's building today—it's about the foundation he's laying for a better tomorrow.

The Road Ahead

As Rodez continues to grow, the legacy of Aman Singh is a story in motion—one that's being written with every new project, every bold decision, and every life he touches. From the tech hubs of Bangalore to the cultural heart of Lucknow, Rodez is expanding its reach, its impact, and its vision for the future.

This is not just a company's journey; it's a celebration of ambition, innovation, and the power of dreaming big. The legacy of Aman and Rodez is a reminder that the greatest stories are not just about what's been achieved—they're about what's yet to come.

This is **The Legacy in Motion**—and it's only getting started.

Suruchi's Note:

Why I Decided to Write "The King ofMagnetic dreams " Dreams"

When I crossed path with Aman Singh, I was struck not just by his success, but by his story. He didn't come from a big city, nor did he attend one of those Technical colleges people often associate with success. As a child, he wasn't an academic superstar, and he didn't follow the traditional route of studying abroad or getting into IIT or IIM. Yet, he built something extraordinary. His journey made me realize that success doesn't need an elite background, fancy degrees, or a head start—it needs dreams and determination.

Aman's story isn't just about a company—it's about the power of chasing dreams, no matter where you start from. I decided to write *The King of Magnetic Dreams* because I believe his story can inspire anyone who has ever doubted themselves. It's a story of resilience, belief, and the power of willpower that can help you achieve anything.

1. Success Isn't About the Elite Background

Aman didn't have the luxury of attending Ivy League schools or studying abroad in expensive colleges. Instead, he started from a small town and built his empire right here in India. What stands out is his belief that your future isn't defined by where you come from or which college you attend. If you have a clear dream and the courage to work for it, you can go anywhere.

This book is a reminder that success isn't reserved for those with fancy degrees. You can build your dreams, no matter your background.

2. Willpower Is Everything

As a child, Aman wasn't the brightest student. He didn't have the best grades, and many people doubted his potential. But instead of letting this define him, Aman worked hard, stayed curious, and relied on his willpower. He showed me that grades don't determine your future—your attitude, drive, and persistence do.

Through this book, I want people to realize that even if you didn't top your class or go to a big college, your willpower and determination can shape your destiny.

3. Big Dreams Can Start from Small Places

Aman didn't come from a big city or a privileged background, yet he didn't let that hold him back. He started from a small town, but his ambition was as big as any skyscraper. His story is proof that no matter where you start, your dreams can be as big as you want them to be.

This book is for anyone who feels that their current circumstances limit their potential. Just like Aman, you can dream big and work hard to make those dreams a reality, no matter where you're from.

4. You Don't Need to Go Abroad to Achieve Big Things

In today's world, many believe that success only happens when you study or work abroad. But Aman's journey proves that you can build something extraordinary right here in India. He didn't need to go overseas to make his mark. His success shows that the world is full of opportunities, and you can achieve great things from your own roots.

This is an important lesson for anyone who thinks they need to leave their country to find success. The opportunities are right here; you just need to see them and take action.

5. Failure Is Just a Stepping Stone

Aman didn't have a smooth journey. There were plenty of failures, obstacles, and moments of doubt. But instead of letting these setbacks hold him back, he used them as lessons to grow. He believed that failure wasn't the end—it was just another step toward success.

In this book, I want to show you that failure doesn't define you—it refines you. Just because you face challenges doesn't mean you won't succeed. Stay focused on your goal, and you'll find a way to overcome anything.

6. Inspiration for Everyone Who Dreams Big

I wrote *The King of Magnetic Dreams* for everyone who has ever thought they weren't good enough. For those who feel like their background, education, or resources limit their potential. Aman's story is proof that anyone can achieve their dreams, no matter who they are or where they come from.

Whether you're a student uncertain about your future, a professional feeling stuck, or someone who believes their circumstances are too challenging, this book will show you that success is within reach. If you dare to dream big and work hard, there is nothing stopping you.

Final Thoughts

Writing this book was about more than just telling Aman's story—it was about sharing a message of hope. I wanted readers to see that no matter where you start, your dreams are valid. Success doesn't require perfect grades or a famous degree. It requires determination, hard work, and the courage to keep going.

Aman's journey shows that dreams can come true if you believe in them and take action. This book is for anyone who believes in the power of dreams, and for anyone who needs a reminder that they, too, can achieve greatness.

Aman's story is a beacon of hope—a reminder that no matter who you are or where you start, you have the power to create your own success. This book is a tribute to that belief.

Impressions

Our lives are like windows, offering us a choice in how we perceive our challenges and achievements. We can either look through these windows and see the glory of perseverance and the joy of winning, or we can focus on the cracks—the doubts, fears, and weaknesses—that threaten to hold us back. Success is not just about talent or luck; it's built on foundational ingredients like focus, persistence, belief in oneself, and the power of goals. Aman's life and journey exemplify these qualities, offering timeless lessons for anyone chasing their dreams.

1. *Focus: The Lighthouse in Turbulent Times*

Focus is the ability to keep your eyes on the prize, even when distractions and challenges surround you. Aman's unwavering focus on his vision for Rodez has been the cornerstone of his success.

• Building Rodez: When Aman started Rodez, he faced criticism and countless obstacles. Instead of succumbing to doubt, he kept his focus on the goal of creating a company that prioritized client relationships and delivered exceptional results.

• Avoiding Self-Pity: Aman teaches that while setbacks are inevitable, dwelling on them is a waste of time. Instead, he advises picking yourself up quickly, re-aligning your focus, and moving forward.

Lesson: Focus directs your energy toward your goals and prevents you from being distracted by past failures or external negativity.

2. Persistence: The Secret to Never Giving Up

Persistence is the determination to keep going, even when the path is uncertain or filled with obstacles. Aman's journey shows that persistence isn't about avoiding failure but about rising stronger after every setback.

• Believing in the Dream: Aman's belief in his vision kept him going, even when people doubted his abilities or labeled his dreams as impractical.

• Taking Small Steps: He emphasizes the importance of taking even the smallest actions every day to get closer to your dreams.

Lesson: Persistence transforms dreams into reality. As Aman says, "Do whatever you can to ensure you're getting closer to your dream every day."

3. The Power of Goals: A Compass for Success

Aman firmly believes in the transformative power of goals. Without a goal, your energy is scattered. A goal focuses your mind and body on what needs to be achieved, helping you move forward instead of looking back.

• Channelizing Energy: In the early days of Rodez, Aman set clear goals for the company. These goals became the driving force behind every decision, ensuring that he and his team worked toward a shared vision.

• Looking Ahead: Aman teaches that worrying about past losses or what might have been is counterproductive. Instead, channel your energy into actionable steps that lead to success.

Lesson: Goals are like a compass—they keep you on track, even when the journey gets tough.

4. The Power of Will: Recognizing Opportunities

Willpower is the strength to keep moving forward, even when the odds are against you. Aman often says, "Opportunities often come disguised as hard work." Many people fail to recognize these opportunities because they're looking for easy wins.

• Embracing Hard Work: Aman's success with Rodez didn't come from shortcuts but from relentless effort. He teaches that every little bit counts, and consistent effort leads to big results over time.

• Staying Mentally Tough: Aman's mental toughness and inner strength have been his most valuable assets. He believes that while circumstances may change, no one can take away your determination and willpower.

Lesson: Success requires recognizing and seizing opportunities, even when they demand hard work and sacrifice.

5. The Importance of Teamwork: Flying Higher Together

Aman's leadership style reflects his belief in the power of teamwork. He often uses the analogy of a kite:

• "To make a kite fly higher, you need to pull it toward you, not push it." Similarly, people thrive when guided with care, respect, and support.

Teamwork at Rodez:

• Focusing on the Team: Aman's success is not about individual glory but about empowering his team to achieve their best. He prioritizes the team's growth and well-being, knowing that their success leads to collective success.

• Building Relationships: Aman's ability to nurture strong client relationships and foster a collaborative environment within

Rodez has been a key driver of the company's achievements.

Lesson: True leaders focus on their team rather than themselves. Success is a shared journey, and teamwork is the foundation of every great accomplishment.

6. Learning and Evolving: The Growth Mindset

Aman believes that the journey to success is one of constant learning and evolution.

- Learning from Others: He emphasizes the importance of being open to learning from others, adopting new tactics and skills, but never compromising on your dreams.

• Staying Curious: Aman's curiosity and willingness to adapt have allowed him to navigate challenges and seize new opportunities.

Lesson: Growth comes from staying open to new ideas and continuously improving yourself and your strategies.

Reflections on Aman's Journey

Aman's life is a testament to the power of dreams, the strength of will, and the importance of focus and persistence. His journey with Rodez is not just about building a successful business but about inspiring others to believe in themselves and their dreams.

Key Takeaways:

1. Focus on Your Strengths: Don't let self-doubt or criticism derail you. Concentrate on what you can do and build on it.

2. Set Clear Goals: A goal channels your energy and provides direction, helping you stay on track even during tough times.

3. Be Persistent: Success doesn't come overnight. Take consistent actions every day to move closer to your dream.

4. Recognize Opportunities: Opportunities often come in the form of hard work. Embrace them and give your best effort.

5. Value Teamwork: Success is never a solo journey. Build strong relationships and work collaboratively to achieve your goals.

Final Thoughts:

Aman's philosophy teaches us that life's challenges are not roadblocks but opportunities to grow and evolve. He reminds us to believe in our dreams, focus on our goals, and never give up, no matter how tough the journey gets.

As Suruchi reflects, "Our lives are like windows. Choose to look through the glass and see the beauty of what lies ahead, rather than focusing on the cracks. Success is a journey, and every little step counts."

Aman's journey inspires us all to dream big, work hard, and believe in the transformative power of persistence, focus, and teamwork.

You Are Enough

Aman Singh often reflects on the days when self-doubt clouded his vision. There were moments when the voices of the world—full of skepticism, judgment, and criticism—seemed louder than his own belief in himself. But through every twist and turn of his journey, Aman discovered something powerful: the realization that he, as he was, was enough.

The Early Battles with Self-Doubt

In the early stages of his entrepreneurial journey, Aman couldn't help but compare himself to others. He saw people with prestigious degrees, strong networks, and seemingly unlimited resources. He, on the other hand, came from a small town, armed with little more than a dream and a fierce determination to make it come true.

"Do I belong here?" he would sometimes ask himself during where he felt out of place. There were moments when he thought, *Maybe they're right. Maybe I don't have what it takes.*

But then Aman would remind himself of something his parents often said:

"You have everything you need within you to create the life you want. Trust yourself."

Those words became a lifeline.

When Failure Tested Him

The toughest lessons came when failure knocked on his door. He looked at the closed doors and unanswered emails as proof that perhaps he wasn't meant for the big dreams he had envisioned.

But something shifted when he started looking at himself through a different lens. Instead of focusing on what he lacked, he chose to focus on what he had:

- *A strong work ethic.*

- *A relentless desire to learn and grow.*

- *A heart full of dreams and a will to pursue them.*

This mindset helped Aman see that failure didn't mean he wasn't good enough—it was simply a step in the process of becoming better.

Breaking Free from the Pressure to Prove

As Aman's company, Rodez Web Technologies, began to grow, he faced another challenge: the constant pressure to prove his worth. Whether it was to clients, competitors, or even himself, Aman felt like he was in an endless race to show the world that he deserved success.

But one day, something shifted. Aman realized that the only person he truly needed to prove himself to was himself.

"I don't need to meet someone else's definition of success," he thought. "I define my own path, and I'm enough as I am."

From that moment, Aman stopped chasing validation from others and started focusing on creating value and impact.

A Lesson for Everyone

Through his journey, Aman learned a truth that he now shares with anyone who doubts themselves:

- **You don't need to be perfect to succeed.**

- **You don't need to have all the answers before you start.**

• **You don't need someone else's approval to follow your dreams.**

What you need is to believe in your own ability to grow, to learn, and to adapt. The skills, resources, and opportunities will come when you take that first step with faith in yourself.

Aman's Words of Wisdom

Aman often tells people, *"The world will always have opinions about you—what you can do, what you can't do, and what you should or shouldn't try. But their opinions aren't your reality. The only voice that truly matters is the one inside you. Listen to it. Trust it. Because you are enough."*

Why You Are Enough

Aman's story is proof that you don't need to have it all figured out to make your dreams come true. You don't need to have every resource, every connection, or every answer. What you need is to believe in your potential and take action, one step at a time.

You are enough—not because you have all the answers, but because you have the ability to find them. You are enough—not because the world says so, but because you decide to believe in yourself.

This chapter is a reminder for every reader of *The King of Magnetic Dreams*: no matter where you are or what challenges you face, you are enough.

The Power Of Starting Small

How Small Beginnings Lead to Big Dreams

When we think of success, we often imagine a grand, overnight transformation. We picture someone suddenly achieving greatness—like a business booming, a dream coming true, or a life-changing moment. But in reality, success doesn't usually happen that way. It begins in small, quiet steps that add up over time.

Small Beginnings Have Big Potential

The power of starting small lies in the belief that even the tiniest seed can grow into something incredible. Think of a tree. It doesn't start as a towering giant. It begins as a small, fragile seed. But with time, care, and persistence, it grows strong and tall, providing shade and shelter to everything around it.

Your dreams are like that seed. They may start small—maybe it's just an idea or a hope. But when you nourish that idea with effort, patience, and hard work, it has the potential to grow beyond what you can imagine.

Why Starting Small is So Powerful

1. It Builds Momentum

The first step is always the hardest. But once you take it, the next one becomes easier. As you continue, you gain confidence and clarity, and what once seemed impossible starts to feel possible.

Small progress builds momentum, and over time, it propels you forward in ways you never expected.

2. It Teaches You to Learn and Adapt

Starting small allows you to learn. When you start with something manageable, you have the opportunity to make mistakes, learn from them, and adjust your approach. Each small step teaches you valuable lessons that prepare you for bigger challenges ahead.

3. It Reduces Fear and Overwhelm

Big dreams can feel overwhelming. The bigger the goal, the scarier it can seem. But when you start small, the pressure feels lighter. Instead of worrying about a massive outcome, you focus on the next small task in front of you. Over time, those tasks stack up, and what once felt impossible becomes a reality.

4. It Creates a Solid Foundation

Starting small allows you to build a strong foundation. Think of it like building a house. You don't start with the roof—you start with the foundation. The same applies to your dreams. When you take the time to get the basics right, the bigger structures you build will be stronger and more stable.

5. It Proves That Progress is More Important Than Perfection

Starting small teaches you to focus on progress, not perfection. No one ever built something great by waiting for the "perfect moment" or having the "perfect plan." It's the steady, consistent effort that makes the difference. When you start small, you embrace the idea that every step forward is a success, no matter how small.

The Journey from Small to Big

Many of the most successful people and organizations today started with humble beginnings. They didn't have endless resources, fancy degrees, or grand networks. They had an idea, a vision, and the courage to start, no matter how small the first step was. What set them apart wasn't a huge leap, but the consistent effort they put into their small beginnings.

What's important to remember is that even the most successful people and companies had humble beginnings. They started with a small spark, and over time, they built something extraordinary. It wasn't magic. It was patience, hard work, and the belief that small steps could lead to something big.

Your Dreams Are Worth Starting Small

No matter where you are in life or how big your dreams are, starting small is the key to making them a reality. The important thing is not to get overwhelmed by the size of your goal, but to take that first step, no matter how small it may seem.

So, if you have a dream, don't wait for the perfect moment to start. Don't wait until you have all the resources or everything is lined up perfectly. Start with what you have, and take that first step. Because that small step is where the magic begins.

Remember: **Small beginnings are the foundation for great success.** Keep going, stay focused, and trust the process. With time, effort, and persistence, your small dreams can grow into something big and beautiful.

Goals

Your Guide to Greatness

Goals are like the lighthouse in a dark sea—they guide you, keep you focused, and push you to keep moving forward, no matter how rough the journey gets. They give our lives direction, purpose, and meaning. Without goals, life feels aimless, but with them, even the impossible starts to feel achievable.

Let's dive into how powerful goals can be and how they can transform lives, inspire people, and lead to success.

1. Goals Give You a Clear Path

Imagine setting out on a journey without knowing where you're going. Sounds confusing, right? Goals are the map that show you the way. They help you decide what to focus on and what to leave behind.

• **Clarity:** Goals tell you exactly what you want to achieve. Instead of being all over the place, you know where your energy needs to go.

• **Focus:** With a clear goal, distractions won't sway you because you know what really matters.

Example: Think about a student preparing for exams. Their goal of scoring good marks keeps them focused, helping them ignore unnecessary distractions like social media or parties.

2. Goals Keep You Motivated

When you have a goal, it's like having a fire inside you. It keeps you excited, even on the hardest days. Goals give you a reason to get up every morning and work hard, even when it feels tough.

• **Motivation:** A clear goal keeps reminding you why you started, pushing you to keep going.

• **Commitment:** When you set a goal, it's like making a promise to yourself. You stay accountable and committed.

Example: An entrepreneur building a business stays motivated through long hours and challenges because their goal of creating something meaningful drives them forward.

3. Goals Turn Dreams Into Reality

We all have dreams—big and small. But dreams alone won't take us anywhere. Goals are what turn those dreams into plans, and plans into action.

• **Actionable Steps:** Goals help you break down your dreams into small, doable tasks.

• **Measurable Progress:** They let you see how far you've come and what's left to achieve.

Example: If you dream of starting your own company, a goal like saving a specific amount of money or learning certain skills helps make that dream real.

4. Goals Build Your Strength and Resilience

Chasing goals isn't always easy. There will be obstacles, failures, and tough days. But that's when goals become even more powerful—they teach you to be strong and keep moving forward.

• **Overcoming Challenges:** Goals push you to find solutions instead of giving up.

• **Personal Growth:** Every step toward your goal makes you stronger and more confident.

Example: A marathon runner faces pain, exhaustion, and self-doubt. But their goal of crossing the finish line keeps them going, teaching them resilience along the way.

5. Goals Teach You Discipline and Focus

Goals keep you focused on what truly matters. They teach you to avoid shortcuts and distractions, helping you stay disciplined.

• **Prioritization:** Goals make you understand what's important and what isn't.

• **Delayed Gratification:** They show you the value of hard work and patience by teaching you to work today for rewards tomorrow.

Example: Someone saving money for their dream home learns to cut back on unnecessary expenses, staying disciplined because their goal is more important than temporary pleasures.

6. Goals Bring a Sense of Achievement

There's no better feeling than reaching a goal you've worked hard for. It's not just about the result; it's about knowing you gave your best and made progress.

• **Confidence Boost:** Every achieved goal makes you believe in yourself more.

• **Momentum:** Success builds on success. Once you achieve one goal, you're motivated to aim for bigger ones.

Example: A team finishing a big project on time feels proud and confident, ready to take on the next challenge with even more enthusiasm.

7. Goals Bring People Together

In organizations or teams, shared goals create unity. They make people work together, aligning their efforts toward a common vision.

• **Team Spirit:** Goals encourage collaboration and make everyone feel like they're part of something meaningful.

• **Collective Success:** Achieving a shared goal strengthens bonds and builds trust among team members.

Example: A company launching a new product successfully brings its marketing, development, and sales teams together with one shared mission.

8. Goals Make Life Meaningful

Life is not just about passing time—it's about living with purpose. Goals give you that purpose. They help you build something meaningful, something you can look back on and feel proud of.

• **Legacy:** Goals ensure your actions make a lasting impact.

• **Fulfillment:** They align your daily actions with your dreams, giving you a sense of accomplishment.

Example: A person working toward funding education for underprivileged children finds deep meaning in their efforts, knowing they're changing lives.

How to Make Goals Work for You

1. **Be Clear:** Define exactly what you want to achieve. Don't make it vague; make it specific.

2. **Start Small:** Break big goals into smaller, manageable steps.

3. **Stay Flexible:** If things don't go as planned, adjust your approach but never lose sight of the goal.

4. **Celebrate Wins:** Every milestone matters. Celebrate small victories to stay motivated.

5. **Keep Your Eye on the Prize:** Stay focused on the end result, no matter how tough the journey gets.

Final Thoughts

Goals are more than just targets—they're the bridge between where you are and where you want to be. They guide you, motivate you, and help you grow. Whether it's a personal goal like learning a new skill or a big dream like building a successful business, the power of goals can turn the ordinary into the extraordinary.

Set a goal today, work toward it with all your heart, and watch how it transforms your li Every step you take brings you closer to the person you're meant to be and the legacy you're meant to leave behind.

Dare To Dream

Dreaming is not just about imagining a better future; it's about believing that the future you imagine can be real. To dare to dream means to step beyond what feels safe and familiar, and to picture something bigger than yourself—something extraordinary. It's about allowing your heart to envision possibilities that might seem out of reach, yet choosing to pursue them anyway.

Dreams are not just for the lucky or talented. They are for everyone who has the courage to believe in them. The size of your dreams doesn't depend on where you come from or what you have. It depends on your willingness to think beyond the limits of what seems possible. Even the smallest spark of an idea can grow into something incredible if you give it the attention and effort it deserves.

But let's be honest: dreaming big isn't easy. It takes courage to dream because dreams come with risks. You might fail. People might doubt you. You might doubt yourself. There will be challenges along the way—obstacles that make the journey feel overwhelming. But here's the truth: every great achievement, every innovation, and every success story began with a dream. And every dreamer faced fear and failure at some point. What set them apart was their refusal to give up.

When you dare to dream, you open the door to growth. You start to see potential in yourself that you never realized was there. You begin to break down mental barriers and discover strength you didn't know you had. Dreaming pushes you to take risks, to work harder, and to believe in your own ability to create change.

The power of a dream lies not just in imagining it but in acting on it. Dreams don't come true overnight. They require focus, persistence, and belief, even when the path feels uncertain.

But with every step forward, you get closer to making them real.

So, dare to dream—not small, easy dreams, but bold and challenging ones. Dream about the life you want to live, the person you want to become, and the impact you want to make. Your dream might feel impossible today, but with courage, hard work, and a clear purpose, you can turn it into reality.

Remember, the world has been shaped by dreamers who were brave enough to imagine something new and determined enough to bring it to life. Their stories prove that when you dare to dream, anything is possible. And now, it's your turn. What will you dream of? And more importantly, what will you do to make it happen?

The Power Within

As this journey reaches its final pages, *The King of Magnetic Dreams* reveals its most profound truth: the power to create an extraordinary life lies within each of us. This story is more than a chronicle of success—it is a testament to the forces of **manifestation** and **resilience**, timeless principles that turn impossible dreams into reality.

The protagonist's journey wasn't about luck or privilege. It was about discovering and mastering the hidden potential within—the ability to dream vividly, believe unshakably, and persevere relentlessly. It's a story that reflects the possibilities in all of us, reminding us that no matter where we begin, we have the power to shape where we end up.

Manifestation: The Dream That Sparks Change

Every great achievement begins with a dream—a spark that ignites the imagination and fills the heart with possibility. But dreaming isn't just about wishful thinking; it's about creating a mental blueprint for the life you desire.

In this story, the power of manifestation is woven into every step of the journey:

• **A Vision That Leads the Way**: The dreamer dared to see beyond the present, painting a vivid picture of a future that seemed out of reach. That vision became a guiding light, shining even in the darkest moments.

• **Belief as a Superpower**: The dreamer didn't just hope for change; they believed in it with every fiber of their being. That belief was magnetic, pulling opportunities, people, and circumstances into alignment with their vision.

• **Action Meets Intention**: Dreams alone are not enough. This story shows that manifestation requires action—taking steps, no matter how small, toward the goal. Each action builds momentum, turning the dream into something tangible and real.

The lesson is clear: your mind is the most powerful tool you have. When you focus your thoughts, emotions, and actions on a dream, you awaken a magnetic force that draws the life you desire closer with every step.

Resilience: The Strength to Rise, Again and Again

Yet even the brightest dreams face storms. Challenges and failures are inevitable, but what defines us is how we respond to them. The journey in *The King of Magnetic Dreams* is a masterclass in resilience—showing what it means to face adversity head-on and emerge stronger every time.

• **Failures Are Just Detours**: In the story, every failure becomes a lesson. Each setback, rejection, or moment of doubt serves as a stepping stone, pushing the dreamer closer to their ultimate goal.

• **The Power of Perseverance**: Resilience isn't just about surviving challenges—it's about thriving because of them. This story shows how grit and determination transform struggles into triumphs, proving that the harder the climb, the sweeter the victory.

• **Inspiring Others Through Strength**: Resilience isn't only personal. It becomes a source of strength for others, showing that it's possible to rise, no matter how hard the fall.

The story reminds us that every challenge shapes us, every failure refines us, and every moment of doubt tests our belief in ourselves. Resilience is the heart that refuses to quit, the spirit that dares to keep moving forward.

A Universal Message

As you close this book, take a moment to reflect. The journey you've just read isn't only about one person—it's about the possibilities that exist within each of us. This isn't just a story; it's a mirror, a reminder of what we're capable of when we embrace the power of our dreams and our ability to endure.

- **You Hold the Power to Manifest**: Your dreams are magnetic. What you truly desire is already drawn to you—it's waiting for you to believe in it fully and take the steps to bring it to life.

- **You Possess Unbreakable Resilience**: No matter how many times life knocks you down, you have the strength to rise again. Every obstacle is preparing you for the greatness you're destined to achieve.

The dreamer in this story didn't have anything you don't already possess. The same ability to dream big, believe deeply, and persevere boldly is within you. The difference lies in how you choose to use it.

Epilogue

Your Dreams, Your Journey

As we reach the end of Aman's story, one undeniable truth stands out: life is a journey shaped by the dreams we dare to pursue. Aman began as an ordinary individual, someone who played by the rules and stuck to the safety of routines. Like so many of us, he felt the weight of expectations and the fear of stepping into the unknown. Yet, hidden deep within him was a spark—a dream that refused to die, no matter how much he tried to suppress it.

This epilogue isn't just about Aman's journey; it's an invitation for you to reflect on your own life. What dream lies dormant within you? What is it that excites you, scares you, and makes your heart race at the thought of pursuing it? Aman's story shows us that dreams are not just fanciful wishes—they are the essence of what makes life meaningful.

The Courage to Dream

Aman's life reminds us that the first and most important step in pursuing a dream is finding the courage to dream in the first place. For years, Aman ignored the quiet voice inside him that whispered of possibilities. He was caught up in the demands of everyday life, settling for comfort over growth.

But when he finally listened to that voice, something changed. He realized that dreams are not reserved for the lucky or the extraordinary. They are for anyone who dares to believe in them. This is a powerful lesson for all of us: dreaming is not about having all the answers; it's about taking the first step even when the path ahead is unclear.

The Journey of Growth

The road to chasing dreams is rarely smooth. Aman faced failures that tested his patience and moments of doubt that made him question everything. There were times when he felt like giving up, wondering if his efforts were worth it. But every setback brought him closer to understanding the true nature of growth.

Failures became stepping stones. Mistakes turned into lessons. And every small victory, no matter how insignificant it seemed, fueled his determination. This journey transformed Aman—not just in what he achieved but in who he became. He discovered resilience, built confidence, and developed a mindset that saw challenges as opportunities rather than obstacles.

This is the heart of Aman's story: the dream itself is only part of the journey. The real reward lies in the person you become along the way.

The Power of Belief

Aman's transformation was driven by one crucial factor: belief. Belief in his dream, belief in the process, and most importantly, belief in himself. It wasn't easy. Like anyone else, Aman had moments when his fears seemed stronger than his faith. But he learned that belief is a muscle—it grows stronger the more you use it.

Through his journey, Aman discovered that believing in your dreams has a magnetic power. It pulls you forward, even when the road gets tough. It inspires others to believe in you and in their own potential. And most importantly, it reminds you that you are capable of achieving far more than you think.

Dreams That Inspire Others

Aman's journey didn't just change his life; it became a beacon of hope for others. By daring to chase his dreams, he inspired countless people around him to take action on their own. His story showed them that success is not reserved for a select few—it's available to anyone willing to put in the effort, face their fears, and stay committed.

Aman became a mentor, sharing his experiences and guiding others who were just starting their journeys. His dream became bigger than himself—it became a movement, a ripple effect of inspiration and change. This is a powerful reminder that when you chase your dreams, you not only transform your own life but also impact the lives of those around you.

Redefining Success

For Aman, success wasn't about fame, money, or accolades. It was about waking up each day with purpose, knowing he was living a life true to himself. It was about the freedom to create, to inspire, and to grow. And it was about leaving a legacy—not in the form of material wealth, but in the lives he touched and the dreams he helped others realize.

This redefinition of success is one of the most important lessons from Aman's journey. It reminds us that true success is not about what we achieve but about who we become and the impact we make along the way.

Your Story Begins Now

As you close this book, remember that Aman's story isn't unique. It is a reflection of the universal truth that every one of us has the potential to live a life of meaning and purpose. The key lies in daring to dream, taking that first step, and staying committed even when the road gets tough.

This epilogue is not an ending—it's a beginning. It's an invitation for you to look within and rediscover the dreams that make your heart beat faster. Maybe it's a dream you've carried since childhood, or maybe it's something new that excites you. Whatever it is, let Aman's story remind you that it's never too late to start.

Dreams are not about perfection; they are about progress. They are not just about achieving a goal but about the journey of becoming the best version of yourself.

So, take the leap. Dare to believe in your dreams. Let them guide you, challenge you, and transform you. Because just like Aman, you too can become the king—or queen—of your magnetic dreams.

Ending

The King of Magnetic Dreams

As we close the pages of *The King of Magnetic Dreams*, it's not the end of the story—it's the beginning of your own journey. The message that I hope you take from this book is simple: dreams are not bound by your background, your past, or your circumstances. They are born in your mind and fueled by your willpower, persistence, and the courage to keep moving forward, even when the world tells you otherwise.

Aman Singh's story isn't just about building a business or achieving personal success—it's a testament to the power of believing in something greater than yourself. It's about understanding that every setback, every failure, and every challenge is simply a stepping stone toward something bigger.

Remember:

1. **Your background doesn't define your future.** No matter where you start, your dreams are valid. Aman didn't come from wealth or privilege, but that didn't stop him from creating something that now impacts thousands of people.

2. **Your willpower is your greatest asset.** You don't need perfect grades, an Ivy League degree, or a prestigious network to succeed. What you need is determination. You need the courage to take that first step, even when the road ahead seems unclear.

3. **Small beginnings can lead to extraordinary outcomes.** Don't underestimate the power of starting small. Like a tiny seed, your efforts, when nurtured with belief and passion, can grow into something truly remarkable.

4. Failure is not the end. It's simply a part of the journey. Every failure brings with it a lesson, a chance to improve and grow. Just as Aman turned his setbacks into success, so can you.

Now, it's your turn.

Take this story as a spark to ignite your own dreams. Don't wait for the "right" moment or the "perfect" circumstances. The time to begin is now. What matters most is your belief in your dreams and the dedication to make them a reality, no matter how long the path may seem.

This book was never just about Aman. It's about *you*. It's about all the dreamers, the doers, and the believers out there who are ready to turn their dreams into something extraordinary.

The world needs more people like you—people who are willing to dream big, to work hard, and to create change.

So, what's your dream? And what are you going to do today to make it happen?

Your legacy, like Aman's, is waiting to be written. The journey of a lifetime begins with that first, bold step.

An Invitation to Your Own Magnetic Journey

As this book ends, your own story begins. What dreams are calling to you? What visions make your heart race? What challenges lie in your path, waiting to shape you into the person you're meant to become?

The message of *The King of Magnetic Dreams* is simple yet profound: you are the author of your life. You have the power to dream, to believe, and to rise. You have the ability to turn your challenges into opportunities, your failures into lessons, and your dreams into reality.

This book is a spark. Let it ignite something within you. Let it remind you that your journey is worth it, your dreams are worth it, and above all, *you* are worth it.

Now, as you step into your own story, remember: the world is waiting for your magnetic dreams. What will you create? How will you rise? The choice, as always, is yours.

The King of Magnetic Dreams is only the beginning.